The South Tower, Tutbury

THE CASTLES AND MOATED MANSIONS OF STAFFORDSHIRE

Mike Salter

FOLLY PUBLICATIONS

ACKNOWLEDGEMENTS

Except for the old photograph showing the west side of Caverswall Castle, which is reproduced by courtesy of the Staffordshire County Museum, the photographs in this book were taken by the author between 1969 and 1996, whilst the old prints are reproduced from originals in his possession. He also drew the map and all the plans and other drawings. The plans are to a set of common scales, i.e. 1:400, 1:1250, and 1:2000. Thanks are due to Paul Adkins for help with setting up a new computer system, to Max Barfield for help with transport and the loan of a camera, and to Marjorie Salter, who did the proof reading.

AUTHOR'S NOTES

This book is a revised new edition with a number of extra illustrations of a book originally released in March 1989 under the title The Castles of Staffordshire and the West Midlands County. This edition uses the pre-1974 Staffordshire boundaries. Material for the Warwickshire part of the West Midlands County used in the original edition can be found in another book in this series, The Castles and Moated Mansions of Warwickshire, published in 1992 and still available.

The books in this series (see list inside the back Cover) are intended as portable field guides giving as much information as possible in volumes of modest size, weight and price. The aim is to mention where known, owners, tenants, or custodians who erected parts of the fabric of a described building, or were the first or last of a line to hold an estate or title. Other occupants of historical interest are mentioned but there is no attempt to give complete geneological details of each landed family, nor are there any stories about ghosts or the like. The books are meant to be used in conjunction with Ordnance Survey 1:50,000 scale maps. Grid references are given in the gazetteer together with a coding system indicating which buildings can be seen by the public. The codes are F - free access at any time; H - buildings used as hotels, restaurants, etc; O - opened to the public by private owners or local councils, usually with a fee payable; V - not open but visible at close range from a public open space, path, road, churchyard, etc. Each level of a building is called a storey in this book, the first storey being the lowest and more or less at courtyard level unless specifically mentioned as otherwise. All dimensions are given in metres. For those who need to convert to feet 3 metres is fractionally under 10 feet. Dimensions quoted are usually external at or near ground level but above the plinth if there is one.

ABOUT THE AUTHOR

Mike Salter is 43 and has been a professional writer and publisher under the name Folly Publications since he went on the Government Enterprise Allowance scheme for unemployed people in 1988. He is particularly interested in the planning and layout of medieval buildings and has a huge collection of plans of churches and castles he has measured during tours (mostly by bicycle and motorcycle) of England, Ireland, Scotland and Wales since 1968. Wolverhampton born and bred, since 1990 Mike has lived in an old cottage beside the Malvern Hills. His other interests include walking, model railways, board games, morris dancing, and playing percussion instruments.

Original edition (ISBN 1 871731 02 X) published March 1989, reprinted August 1993
Folly Publications, Folly Cottage, 151 West Malvern Rd, Malvern, Worcs, WR14 4AY
Printed by Aspect Design, 89 Newtown Rd, Malvern, Worcs, WR14 2PD

Alton Castle

CONTENTS

A map of Staffordshire appears inside the front cover.

For details of public access see opposite page.

INTRODUCTION

This book is essentially about medieval buildings which illustrate the old saying that an Englishman's home is his castle. Those here described either had a genuine dual purpose as both fortress and private residence, or were basically domestic buildings which were given features traditionally associated with defence as a means of displaying the owner's rank, prestige, wealth and power.

The concept of a privately owned fortress-cum-residence was little known in England prior to the invasion of William, Duke of Normandy in 1066. After becoming King of England he established within it the feudal system in which tenants-in-chief held directly from the king numerous units of land called manors in return for military service. The tenants-in-chief then gave many of their manors to knights on the same basis. The slender veneer of French-speaking Normans consolidated their hold on these lands inhabited by the Saxon populace by building themselves fortified residences which they called castles. Some Saxons, however, managed to remain in positions of power alongside the new Norman lords. Edwin, Earl of Mercia, who ruled much of what became the county of Staffordshire did not oppose Duke William in 1066, although his earldom was abolished after he rebelled and was defeated and killed in 1071. A Saxon called Richard Chenvin was appointed to the important post of Custodian of the royal forest of Cannock, and the Bagot family, long of importance in Staffordshire, are said to be of Saxon rather than Norman origin.

King William came to the midlands in 1069 and 1070 to put down rebellions. On the latter occasion he had a castle built beside the town of Stafford. This has now vanished but analogy with the contemporary castles at Warwick and Shrewsbury suggests that it was constructed of earth and wood rather than stone. A circular ditch would have been dug and the materials piled in the middle to raise a mound or motte on which was erected a timber house or tower set within a small stockaded court. The mound summit would have been reached by a long flight of steps up from an enclosure or bailey stockaded rampart and a ditch enclosing a scattering of wooden buildings including a hall, a chapel, a granary, barns, workshops, and stores.

After abolishing the earldom of Mercia, King William gave a large estate west of Stafford to his hereditary standard bearer Roger de Toeni. His son Robert took the surname de Stafford and founded the noble family of that name, destined to become Dukes of Buckingham. At the time of the Domesday survey of 1086 Robert de Stafford was the chief landholder in Staffordshire after the king. It was probably soon afterwards that Robert raised the fine motte and bailey castle on an eminence 2km west of Stafford as his fortress, administrative centre and chief residence. At this time the Earl of Shrewsbury held much land in Staffordshire although his castles were mostly in Shropshire. Henry de Ferrers held a large estate in NE Staffordshire and Derbyshire centred on a castle at Tutbury, while William Fitz-Ansculf held what is now called the Black Country with a castle at Dudley. Robert Marmion built the castle at Tamworth, and the Earl of Chester, who also held large estates in Staffordshire may have built the earthworks at Chartley by 1100. These castles were of the type described above, adapted according to the terrain and the resources available. Most had one or two outer baileys in addition to the basic motte and bailey plan. The other castles of this type in Staffordshire are likely to be early or mid 12th century. Newcastle-under-Lyme had a motte and a single bailey on a low-lying site with water defences, while at Audley, Biddulph, and perhaps Ashley, natural hills were shaped into low mounds without adjoining baileys.

Contemporary chronicles and documents show that castles played an important part in the conflicts between King Stephen (1135-54) and the supporters of Henry I's daughter Matilda, who included the Earl of Chester and the Paganels, now lords of Dudley. Their castles saw much action. In 1138 Robert de Ferrers of Tutbury was created Earl of Derby after supporting King Stephen at the battle of Northallerton.

The motte at Tutbury

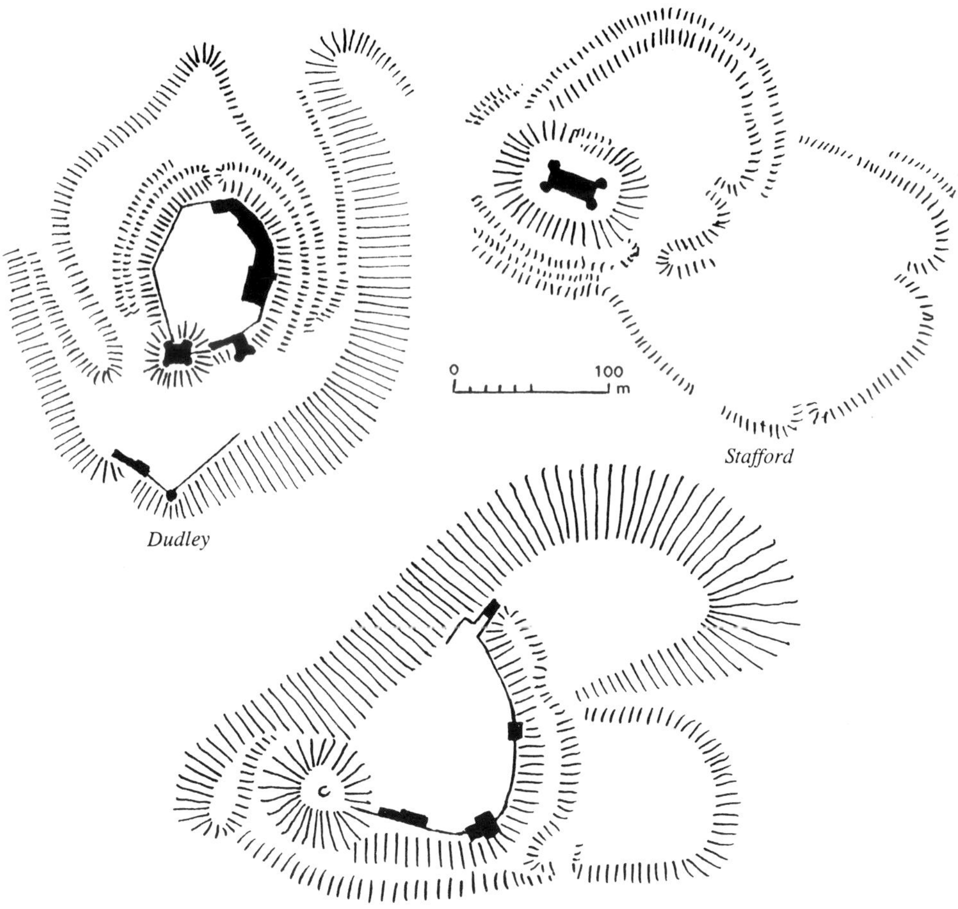

Plans of Norman castle earthworks in Staffordshire

Timber is vulnerable to accidental or deliberate destruction by fire, and soon rots away when in constant contact with the soil. Gradually timber structures were rebuilt in mortared stone. In Staffordshire the only surviving stonework likely to be earlier than the 1170s is at Tamworth. There the wall bearing the pathway up the east side of the mound is faced with herringbone masonry which must be of c1100-50. The shell keep, a thick stone substitute for the original palisade on the edge of the mound summit, is somewhat later, and may be 13th century. Within it would have once been lean-to timber buildings replacing the original free-standing wooden house or tower. Some of the functions of the latter may have been taken over by the contemporary square tower projecting slightly from the shell wall towards the approach.

On his accession in 1154 Henry II began to restore the balance between royal and baronial castles by a policy of keeping some confiscated castles in his own hands, building new ones, and demolishing those belonging to barons of dubious loyalty. It was probably he who built a rectangular stone tower keep at Newcastle-under-Lyme. Like the keep he built in the 1160s at Bridgnorth it would have had pilaster buttresses at the corners and an entrance above ground level leading into the main living room or hall. A spiral stair in a corner by the entrance would have led down to a dark cellar and up to a private room and the battlements. It has vanished but a few courses remain of what was probably a smaller copy of it built on one side of the mound summit at Stafford.

The rebellion led by the king's sons in 1173-4 gave Henry II a new opportunity to destroy the castles of rebel barons, including those of Tutbury and Dudley. Their owners were only allowed repossession after total submission and payment of heavy fines. Tutbury was soon rebuilt and certainly had a stone chapel by the 1190s and probably also a shell keep like that of Tamworth, but rather smaller. The de Verduns' began the stone castle of Alton at this time, but Richard I's hunting lodge at Stourton and the Bishop of Lichfield's house at Eccleshall were at this period still timber structures of modest defensive strength.

From his succession as Earl of Chester in 1180 until his death in 1232, Ranulph de Blunderville was one of the most powerful nobles of his time. As a reward for supporting the crown in the troubled period 1214 to 1218 he was entrusted with the keeping of the strongholds of Newcastle-under-Lyme and Peveril in Derbyshire. He had possession of Lancashire from 1216, and in 1217 gained the earldom of Lincoln. He was on crusade in the Holy Land from May 1218 until August 1220 and it was on his return, perhaps inspired by the more adavanced stronghold designs there, that he began building the three remarkable castles of Beeston in Cheshire, Old Bolingbroke in Lincolnshire, and Chartley in Staffordshire. The latter has earthworks of probably older origin and had a round tower keep on a mound at one end of a rectangular bailey flanked with five large and very massively constructed round towers, two of which flanked the gateway. The two surviving towers have two levels with fine cross-shaped arrow loops for the discharge of crossbows. In c1225-45 the de Ferrers family erected the now vanished round tower keep at Tutbury between the mound and the gateway shown on a 16th century sketch of the castle.

An associate of Earl Ranulph, Henry de Audley, erected a castle at Heighley spectacularly sited on a sandstone crag like Beeston. Very little remains of it but it is likely that it had a gateway flanked by twin D-shaped towers just like Beeston and Chartley. Nothing now remains of a third castle of this era with round flanking towers erected at Stourton by Henry III's keeper of Kinver Forest. In 1260 a bailey gateway was built at Tamworth with shallow round projections set either side of the entrance passageway, below which was a basement which is now all that remains. The plan form recalls that of contemporary gateways at the royal castles of Dover and Newcastle-upon-Tyne.

Old photograph of Caverswall Castle

By the reign of King John (1199-1216) the building of embattled (crenellated) walls and towers had to be authorised by the Crown. Licences to Crenellate were only granted to a loyal privileged few so that defensive features became a sign of high rank and royal favour. Sometimes they were built for show without any real military function. The many surviving records of licences granted up to the early 16th century help historians to date many embattled houses. Under the terms of licences granted during the last third of the 13th century the manor houses at Caverswall and Eccleshall were made into castles and an embattled wall with gatehouses, corner towers and a formidable ditch was created around the cathedral close at Lichfield. Caverswall and Eccleshall have rectangular courts with walls about 2m thick rising directly from the bottom of what were formerly water-filled moats. Each had polygonal corner towers and a further pair of such towers flanking the gateway. Excavations have now shown that the cathedral close at Lichfield also had such a gateway facing the town. All these structures date from Edward I's reign (1272 1307), a period when Staffordshire enjoyed peace and prosperity and such defences were more for show than a necessity.

Of the same period is the Butler's mansion at Norbury, where there were probably four ranges set around an open court within a wet moat. It was probably never embattled and without flanking towers except for the bartizan of aesthetic rather than military purpose shown perched on one corner in an old print. It was one of the earliest of many later medieval mansions with outer walls only about a metre thick. In such houses the provision of a wet moat crossed only by one trestle bridge leading to a drawbridge, and the fixing of iron grilles or bars on any outer windows within easy reach was deemed adequate to keep out undesirables. The manor houses which were licensed to be crenellated in the 14th century at Bescot, Madeley, and Walsall would have been similar either to Caverswall or Norbury, whilst that at Swynnerton was probably never actually built. It is also uncertain, what if anything, was built at Wolseley after Edward IV granted a licence for the house to be crenellated in 1469.

Crenellation was permitted at Dudley in the 1260s although the existing bailey wall without flanking towers appears to be mostly of a period one or two generations later. The remarkable two storey building with round corner towers on the motte is thought to have been built by Sir John de Somery c1307-20. He is described by contemporaries as a difficult and domineering neighbour and this keep, lying on one of the highest points of the Black Country, was evidently designed to overawe his tenants and neighbours. The plan form recalls a few 13th century keeps in France and Ireland. In England there is nothing quite like it except the much small Ypres Tower on the town walls at Rye, and an earlier square keep at Mulgrave in Yorkshire given round corner towers c1300-10. The modest projection of the corner towers at Dudley gives a plan form closer to the quatrefoil shaped keeps on the mottes of castles of York and Pontefract. Lord Stafford's building of c1347-60 on the motte at Stafford is only vaguely similar to Dudley, being a much longer building with more boldly projecting corner towers. It contained considerably more accommodation than the tower at Dudley where there was only one main room apart from a storage basement. The structure at Stafford has predecessors in the two storey hall houses with corner turrets built at Tarset and Edlingham in Northumberland in the late 13th century. It was perhaps also inspired by the buildings Lord Stafford saw in France during his long years of military service there. The building contract specifically mentions a machicolated parapet, then almost unknown in England, also there were short sections of such a defence at either end of the two wards at Conwy in North Wales. Rather remarkably, although the bailey at Stafford remained in occupation throughout the medieval period, it was never enclosed by a stone curtain wall.

The gatehouse which Thomas, Earl of Lancaster built at Tutbury as part of a general remodelling of the castle is rather modest compared with many contemporary gatehouse, especially that which he erected at Dunstanburgh in Northumberland. More exciting things were to come for Tutbury, most of the curtain walls being built anew during the first half of the 15th century together with two impressive self-contained tower houses. This work, begun for Henry IV and continued by Henry VI and his Queen, Margaret of Anjou, has few parallels in England for it was rare for a much older castle with its plan form set in the 11th century to have its defences so extensively renewed in that period when work at other older castles was confined to repairs and improvements to the domestic buildings rather than long lengths of new curtain. The tower houses, combining the provision of secure and private lordly accommodation with the needs of defence are predecessors of several other great towers built at refuges and status symbols by Edward IV and his leading supporters in the 1470s. The tower of c1500 at Hamstall Ridware is a much humbler echo of these, usable only as a lookout point.

Chartley Castle

The gatehouse at Dudley Castle

Not much has survived of the domestic buildings of the castles and fortified manor houses. Generally the domestic buildings were less durably constructed than the defences. From the medieval period there remain just a 14th century block containing the solar and chapel at Dudley, the base of a chapel at Tutbury, and a much altered range inside the shell keep at Tamworth. Until the Tudor period glass was uncommon in secular buildings and windows were normally closed with shutters so that rooms would have been very dark when the weather was unsuitable for the shutters to be opened. Furnishings would have been sparse, especially when the lord was absent. In order to consume agricultural produce and administer their many manors in person, great lords tended to circulate from one castle or manor house to another, taking their servants and transportable furnishings with them. The Staffords, for example, had other castles at Caus in Shropshire and Newport in Monmouthshire, whilst Tutbury would only have seen occasional royal visits in the 15th century.

Cannon began to make high walls and towers militarily redundant during the 15th century. With the possible exception of some bastions that may have been built at Burton in the 1540s,, no military structures were built in Staffordshire between the 1460s and the Civil War of the 1640s. Domestic buildings continued to be added or remodelled, the hall of c1450-1500 within the shell keep at Tamworth and the splendid apartments of c1550 at Dudley being the most notable. In the early 17th century considerable work was done at Caverswall and Tamworth. Documention is fuller for this period, giving us quite a lot of information about destroyed buildings and their contents. The antiquary John Leland's comment on the buildings he saw c1540 are also useful. Dudley Castle came to prominence as the principal seat of John Dudley, Duke of Northumberland, who in 1553 had the temerity to try and have crowned his Protestant daughter-in-law Lady Jane Grey in preference to Henry VIII's eldest daughter Mary, who was a Catholic. During the reign of Mary's younger sister Elizabeth Tutbury Castle and Chartley Hall were two of the places used for the long imprisonment of Mary, Queen of Scots.

When fighting broke out between Charles I and his Parliament in 1642, many lords and gentry garrisoned and fortified their homes. A majority of them were initially held for the king but Rushall Hall, Caverswall Castle and the town of Leek were held for Parliament. In March 1643 Parliamentary troops captured the cathedral close at Lichfield, losing Lord Brooke in the process. The Royalists in turn lost a leader but gained a victory in the same month when they sallied out of Stafford to forestall a Parliamentary attack on the town and the Earl of Northampton was killed in the resulting battle at Hopton Heath. Prince Rupert recaptured Lichfield Cathedral close in April of that year and Tamworth was also taken by the Royalists, but in May Parliament captured the town of Stafford in a surprise night attack, and Eccleshall castle fell to them in August. Despite these losses the Royalist held the upper hand in north and east Staffordshire until their defeat at Nantwich in Cheshire early in 1644. The Earl of Denbigh captured Rushall Hall for Parliament in May 1644 but he was obliged to give up a siege of Dudley Castle because of problems with paying his troops and the advance of Royalist relief force from Worcester. The Royalists captured Caverswall, Uttoxeter and Burton-on-Trent but their defeat at Naseby in Yorkshire in June ended their hopes of victory. Their remaining garrisons were taken out one by one, although the close at Lichfield held out until July 1646.

To prevent redundant strongholds being used by parties of Royalists intent on continuing the struggle, Parliament made a practice of demolishing those still tenable as fortresses. By the end of 1647 the shell keep at Tamworth was the only notable defensive work in the county that remained unslighted apart from Caverswall, which like Tamworth had had much of its military value reduced by early 17th century rebuilding. By the end of the 17th century country houses had been built on the site of former walls and towers at Eccleshall and Stourton, and in the 18th century a mock-gothic caretaker's house was erected at Tutbury. Stafford and Alton were rebuilt as residences in the 19th century although the work at Stafford was left incomplete and it later fell into ruin again and narrowly escaped demolition in the 1970s. Apart from the keep at Tamworth, now housing a museum, the buildings described in this book are all either very ruinous, have been altered out of recognition since the Civil War, have left behind just a moat, or have vanished altogether.

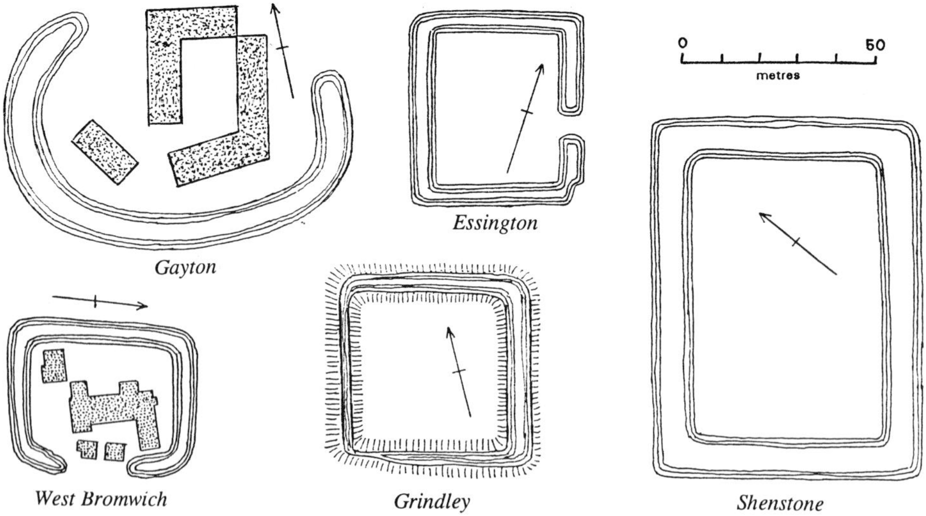

Plans of moated sites in Staffordshire

Scattered across England are moated enclosures marking the sites of former manor houses. Excavations may reveal that some once had stone walls like Norbury but many only had a modest hedge or fence on the inner side of the moat with a timber framed house inside. In some cases the original house has been superseded by a brick or stone farmhouse of the 16th century or later, erected either within the moated platform or just outside it. Despite a number of excavations and a fair amount of research on those sites some questions remain unanswered. Some moats may be 12th century but the majority are of the 13th and 14th centuries. It has been suggested that some moats were constructed in response to periods of unrest in the reigns of Henry III and Edward II. Quite a number appear to have been disused by the 15th century, but others were still being created throughout that period. At Tamworth and Wolverhampton there were late 16th century town houses with, as far as we know, freshly dug moats of that period. Moated sites often occur in groups of two or three fairly close together because of manors being split between heiresses, each of whom required a separate dwelling, or simply because one site was abandoned in favour of a new one elsewhere. Some moats were only occupied for a generation or two. Others have remained in occupation since they were created.

A water filled ditch around a manor house was not necessarily military in purpose. A moat is quite a permanent and efficient boundary for keeping vagrants, wild animals, and malefactors out, and domestic animals, servants and children in. At all periods moats have been appreciated as scenic features and they served as a habitat for fish, eels, and water fowl which together formed a substantial part of the diet of the landed classes. A wet moat could also help to drain land otherwise unsuitable for agriculture or inhabitation. Moats were also used to flush away sewage so a house built within one would require separate source of water for cooking, brewing, and washing. Because of the many uses to which they could be put and perhaps because of the fairly low rank of some of the landowners who created them, moats did not require royal consent of the kind required for the erection of embattled walls and towers. However they still had some sort of function as status symbols since only the lords of manors plus one or two wealthy clergy and trademen could muster sufficient resources to create them.

The words motte and moat clearly have a common origin. Although modern historians normally understand them to mean quite different types of earthwork, this was not the case in the medieval period. A dwelling referred to as being on a "mote" or "motte" in a 14th century document may have been lying upon an 11th or 12th century castle mound of the usual upturned pudding bowl shape, or could just as likely have been on a low platform surrounded by a water filled ditch of more recent origin. Naturally a motte might be regarded as more defensible, but this is often not made clear in old records. One might expect a gradual development from high conical mounds to low rectangular platforms. The low round mound at Weston Jones and the unusually small square platforms which rise above the ground level outside the moats at Ribden and Burnhill Green may perhaps be a transitional type between the motte and the later common form of a rectangular moated platform with sides about 30m to 60m long rising only slightly, if at all, above the ground level outside the moat. Round enclosures with platforms level with the ground outside are uncommon but occur at Gayton and Coppenhall Gorse. Excavation has shown that the latter was occupied in the 14th century. Several sites changed shape when remodelled in later centuries and Eccleshall is known to have had a more rounded form of enclosure prior to the stone curtains being erected. At Blithewood there were concentric outer moats and a number of sites have additional enclosures and/or fishponds.

GAZETTEER OF CASTLES AND MOATED MANSIONS

ALTON CASTLE SK 073425

This little known but spectacularly sited stronghold was built c1170 by Bertram de Verdon. He died while on crusade with Richard I in the Holy Land in the 1190s. According to at least one account the castle was in a neglected state at the time of Theobald de Verdon's death in 1316, after which it passed by marriage to the Furnivals. The surviving remains include work likely to be of c1300 and another account suggests that Theobald rebuilt the castle and perhaps improved its domestic buildings. In 1406 John Talbot obtained Alton on his marriage to the heiress Maud Furnival. He probably put the buildings into a habitable state for occasional use, although he spent much of his time in France, being created Earl of Shrewsbury in 1442 for his services there on behalf of the English Crown. George, 6th Earl was husband of the celebrated Bess of Hardwick, and for a while had custody of the captive Mary, Queen of Scots. Alton Castle was held for King Charles in the Civil War and was later rendered untenable by order of Parliament. In 1787 Charles Talbot, 15th Earl of Shrewsbury began to develop an outlying lodge and its grounds on the other side of the Churnet. His successors continued the work in the 19th century to create the large mansion, now ruined, called Alton Towers. In 1847 the Talbots commissioned Pugin to build a romantic mock castle visible from Alton Towers on the site of the former domestic buildings of the original castle. Seven years earlier Pugin had masterminded the construction of a catholic college on the other side of the moat, and the two form a remarkable group to the north of the church.

The castle lies high above the south side of the ravine of the Churnet. Pugin's building forms a roughly T-shaped plan and stands at the east end of an elliptical court nearly 90m long by 40m wide. A sheer rock face lies below the north side and a steep fall to the west. On the east and south is a sheer sided rock-cut ditch which is 18m wide by 8m deep where a modern bridge crosses it roughly midway along its length. On such a rocky site unsuited to the creation of earthworks the defences must have been of stone from the start, utilising material quarried out of the ditch. The lower parts of a curtain wall about 2m thick remain around the western half of the courtyard. Towards the west end of the south side is the base of a 13th century round tower and further east is an ashlar faced late 12th century rectangular tower about 7.4m wide above a plinth. The upper part of the tower has chamfered off corners and a crossloop and is likely to be of c1300. The prominent relieving arch in the outer face of the tower seems too low to be a blocked gateway and it must be assumed that the entrance lay further east, where the modern bridge gives access to the site.

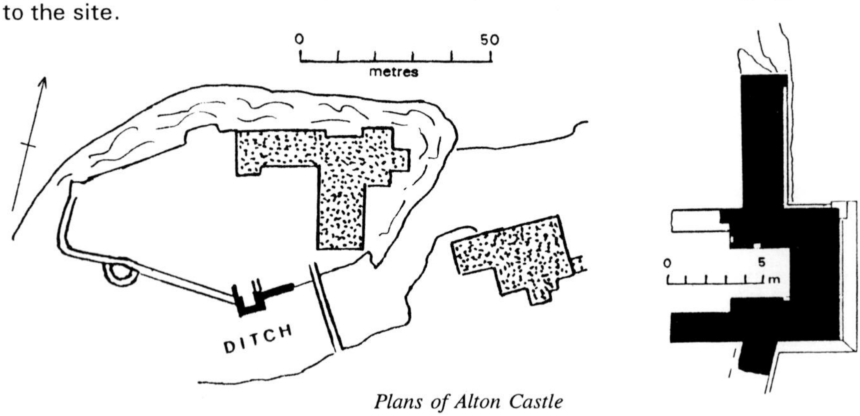

Plans of Alton Castle

Old print of Alton Castle

Alton Castle

Motte at Audley

ASHLEY CASTLE HILL SJ 765375

The wooded hillock called Castle Hill north of the village may be a natural feature used as a Norman motte.

AUDLEY MOTTE SJ 799511 F

On the far side of the A52 from the late medieval parish church is a natural hill which has been adapted to form a low 12th century castle mound with a maximum summit diameter of about 40m. This was the original seat of the de Audley family. Documentary references to this site in 1272-3 and 1275 show it was not immediately abandoned in the 1220s when the family are assumed to have built themselves a stone castle not far away at Heighley, and excavations on the mound revealed a length of thin walling and a coin of the period 1272-1327.

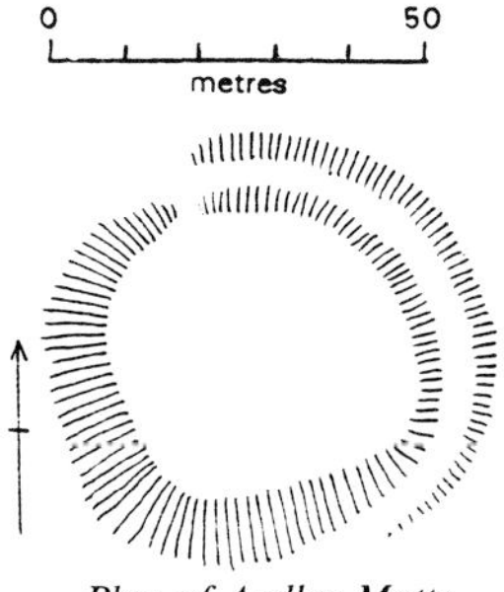

Plan of Audley Motte

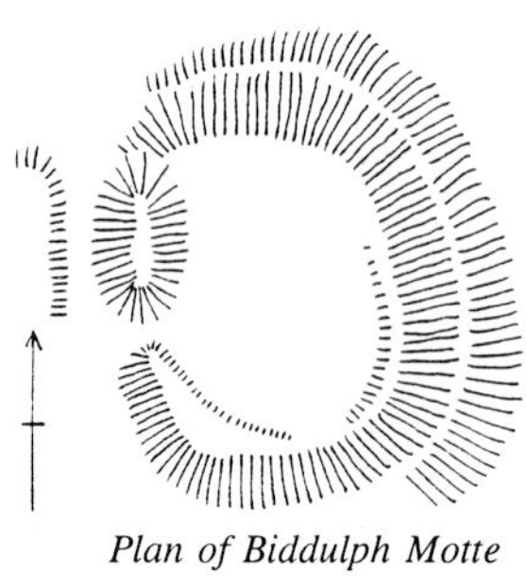

Plan of Biddulph Motte

BARNHURST HALL SJ 894023

In the 16th century the house was held successively by the Leveson and Cresswell families. It was rebuilt in the early 17th century and the dovecot surviving in a new housing estate may be of that period. Traces of the moat survived until the early 1900s.

BESCOT HALL SP 998967

This mansion stood in what is now Pleck Park between the entrance from Bescot Drive and the M6, immediately north of junction 9. The last traces of the moats, which were double on the NW side, finally disappeared c1970. William Hillary held land in Bescot in 1271, and was granted a considerable amount more c1300 by his overlord Roger de Morteyn, lord of Walsall. The moats probably dated from that era, and in 1311 William Hillary was besieged at Bescot by fifty men led by Thomas le Rous. In 1345 William's son Sir Roger Hillary was given licence to crenellate his house at Bescot by Edward III. In the early 15th century Bescot passed to the Mountford family. Sir Simon Mountford was attainted of treason in 1495, but the family recovered Bescot in 1534, and held it until the 1670s. It was then a dwelling of considerable substance, being taxed on 14 hearths in 1666.

Bescot later passed to the Slaneys and several other families. In the 18th century the old hall was demolished and replaced by a new house NE of the moat, over which a bridge was built. The new hall was enlarged in the 1790s, but was leased to tenants by the mid 19th century, and was in turn demolished c1930.

BIDDULPH MOTTE SJ 889594

Excavation of the large conical earthwork at Lea Forge showed that it had been used as a castle mound in the 11th or 12th century. It was strengthened in the late 12th century and the dwelling upon it was rebuilt in the 13th century, and may have remained in use until Biddulph Hall was built in the 16th century. The considerable remains of iron slag showed that there was a forge here in the later medieval period, hence the name Lea Forge.

BLITHFIELD HALL SK 044239

Ralph Bagot married the heiress of the manor of Blithfield in the mid 14th century and in the 1390s Sir John Bagot constructed a new moated mansion, probably of timber. In 1398 he sued the carpenter Robert Stanlowe for 40 marks for faulty work. Nothing remains of this period, the moat having long disappeared and the present building being mostly of 1740 and 1822, but with a late 16th century range on the west side.

BURTON ABBEY SK 251227

The castle of "Burt" mentioned in Domesday is probably an error for Burg or Tutbury. When Burton Abbey was dissolved in 1540 its buildings went to Lord Paget of Beaudesert, along with a licence to crenellate them, an unusual grant at such a late date. Among the Paget papers is a contemporary drawing of the abbey with Tudor type artillery bastions sketched in. The bastions may never have actually been erected but two "field pieces" are recorded at Burton in 1574 on the occasion of the forfeiture of Thomas, 3rd Lord Paget, and the site was garrisoned during the Civil War, being captured by the Royalists in 1644. The original abbey church was wrecked when gunpowder stored within it during the conflict exploded.

CALDEWELLE HALL SP 035991

The surviving circular earthwork may date from the turn of the 13th and 14th centuries when Sir High de Boweles, lord of Rushall, gave "Caldewelle" to his son on the occasion of his marriage and also "bilt and repaired a mansion, and made a moot abowte the mansion".

CAVERSWALL CASTLE SJ 951428 V

A Thomas de Caverswall is recorded in Richard I's reign, but the deep and wide moat, now dry, and the lower parts of the outer walls are the work of Sir William de Caverswall, Sheriff of Shropshire in 1260 and 1269. He was licensed to crenellate his castle at Caverswall in 1275 and lived until 1292. In their present state the walls barely rise above the courtyard, which is roughly a square of about 45m. There are octagonal towers at the corners with another pair flanking the gateway in the middle of the east side. The original main apartments are assumed to have been on the west.

In the 14th century the Caverswalls seem to have preferred to live at High Ercall Hall in Shropshire. At the end of that century the castle passed by marriage to the Montgomery family. The heiress Dorothy Montgomery married Sir Thomas Giffard, heir to Chillington Hall, c1515. Leland calls Caverswall a "pretty pile" c1540, but in Elizabeth's reign it was let to a farmer called Browne and allowed to decay.

In the early 17th century the castle was purchased by the wealthy wool merchant Matthew Craddock. He erected a fine new house c1615 in the northern part of the court, the architect probably being John Smythson, who designed a contemporary block at Bolsover Castle in Derbyshire. The surrounding walls appear to have been rebuilt in the same period. The buttresses at regular intervals on the west, south and east sides, and upper parts of the towers with plain mullioned windows are evidently of this period. Both towers and house were finished with top balustrades, although the main house was given battlements in the 19th century. The Craddocks held the castle for Parliament in the Civil War and it was captured by the Royalists in 1645.

Gateway at Caverswall Castle

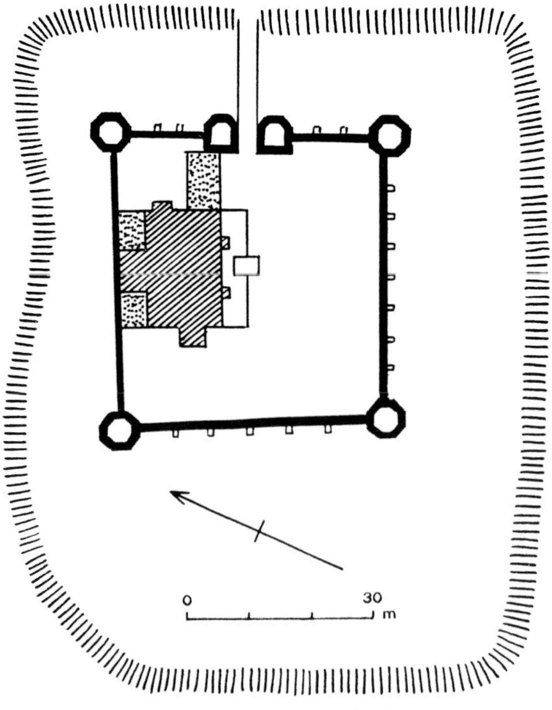

Plan of Caverswall Castle

Caverswall Castle

Old print of Caverswall Castle

CHARTLEY CASTLE AND HALL SK 010285 V

Chartley belonged to the Earls of Chester from the end of the 11th century until 1232, when on Earl Ranulph de Blundeville's death it passed via his daughter Agnes to William de Ferrers, Earl of Derby. The Ferrers family had had an interest (probably as custodians) of the castle in the 12th century, but in 1191-2 it was repaired and garrisoned by the Crown. The earthworks may go back to the 1090s but the stone keep and the bailey walls and towers were built in the 1220s by Earl Ranulph. They were probably in an advanced state on construction in 1223 when the Earl fell out with the young Henry III and was ordered to surrender his many castles. After the defeat of Robert de Ferrers in a fight against the royal forces at Chesterfield in 1266, Henry III gave Chartley to his own younger son Edmund. Robert seized the castle in a surprise night attack and held it until a force was sent to dispossess him. Edward I returned Chartley to Robert in 1274.

SW tower at Charley Castle

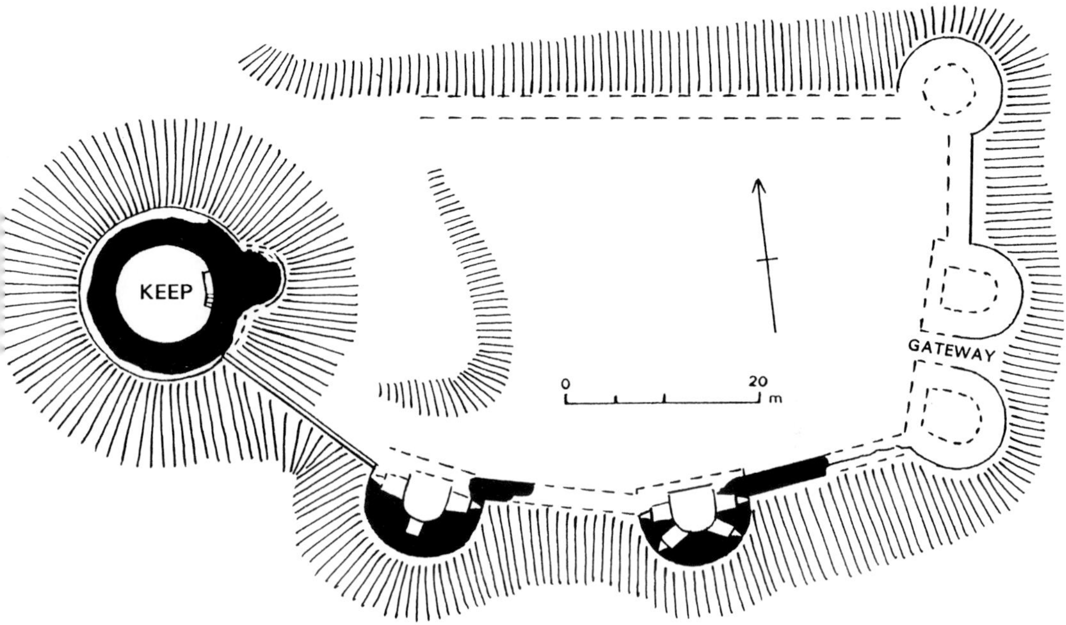

Plan of Chartley Castle

The castle earthworks comprise a small mound at the west end, an inner bailey 70m long by 50m wide, and an outer bailey about 55m square to the east. The parts are separated by ditches and a ditch with an outer bank surrounds the whole site, which lies on a ridge above the Uttoxeter to Stafford road. The motte bears the base of a large round tower keep now only 2m high but originally rising at least 16m high, with two or three storeys. It measures 10.7m in internal diameter with walling 3.7m thick and has towards the bailey slight remains of a projecting round stair turret about 7.8m in diameter. It would appear that the entrance was into this turret at the level of the second storey, from which a staircase led up. The turret was solid below and the basement is now reached from the present wallhead by a stone internal stair, probably a later replacement of an earlier arrangement giving access down only through a trapdoor. The brick walling on the outside of the keep is a relic of when its remains were incorporated into a windmill in the late 18th or early 19th century.

The outer bailey shows no sign of stone defences but the inner bailey was defended by a stone curtain wall of uncertain thickness flanked by five large and massively built flanking towers. Only the defaced bases remain of the NE corner tower and the two towers flanking the gateway at the SE corner, although a higher fragment of the southern gateway tower, with evidence of two embrasures, remained standing in 1970. Not much remains of the curtain wall but there are impressive remains of the D-shaped SW and south towers with respective external diameters of 12.5m and 11.7m and walling up to 4.2m thick. Each has slight traces of the former straight thin inner walls facing the court and evidence of two levels with cross-shaped arrow-loops towards the field. Possibly there may be buried unlit basements although analogy with Beeston suggests not. There is no evidence of staircases or fireplaces in the towers and it must be assumed that the upper levels were reached directly from the court by timber stairs up to doorways in the straight inner walls.

Motte and keep remains, Chartley Castle

After the death of William, 6th baron Ferrers, in 1450, Chartley passed to his daughter Anne and her husband Sir Walter Devereux. He was summoned to Edward IV's first Parliament in 1461 as Baron Ferrers of Chartley and was killed fighting alongside Richard III at Bosworth in 1485. The castle shows no sign of ever having had any domestic buildings and by the 14th century it had probably been abandoned in favour of a timber mansion set within a moat on lower ground to the west. Probably this house lay on the platform 48m long by 29m wide to the north of the present Chartley Hall, a building of 15th century origin lying on a platform with a moat 90m square which broadens out into a pool with two islands towards the castle. Leland c1540 refers to the castle as a ruin and it is unlikely any notable work was carried out on it after the 1270s.

The great grandson of Sir Walter Devereux became Earl of Essex and was a courtier of Elizabeth I. The Queen was entertained at Chartley in 1575. Despite opposition from the 2nd Earl of Essex, Mary, Queen of Scots was confined at Chartley Hall from December 1585 until September 1586, when she was transferred to the castle at Fotheringhay for trial and execution. While at Chartley Mary had been plotting against Elizabeth, her messages to Anthony Babington being smuggled out of the hall in the false bottoms of beer casks. The 2nd Earl of Essex later became a favourite of Queen Elizabeth but after an unsuccessful campaign on her behalf in Ireland he was provoked into a rebellion which led to his execution and attainder in 1601. His son Robert was restored to his estates after James I succeeded to the throne in 1603. Robert took the side of Parliament in the Civil War but neither the hall or the castle appear to have been involved in the conflict. He died childless in 1646 and Chartley passed to his sister's grandson Sir Robert Shirley, created Baron Ferrers of Chartley in 1677, and made Earl Ferrers in 1711. The hall was accidentally burnt down in 1781 and the present house set on the west side of the moated platform is of 1787. The Shirley family remained owners of Chartley until the early 20th century.

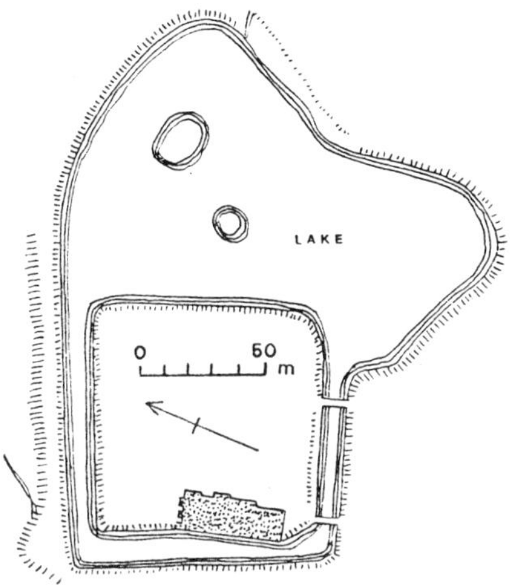

Plan of Chartley Hall Moat

SE tower, Chartley

Section of SE tower, Chartley

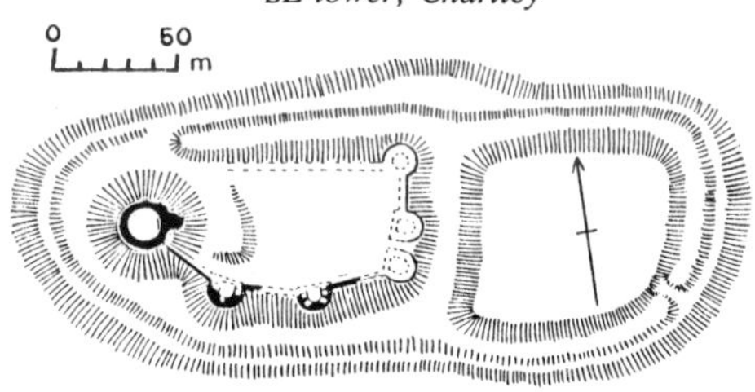

Chartley Castle: plan of earthworks

CHEADLE SK 006413

A former motte by the River Tean at Huntley now lies under a tip.

CHILLINGTON HALL SJ 864068

The curved stretch of water surviving in 1756 was probably a relic of a moat which may have dated back to the time of the Giffard family's original association with the manor in the 12th century. The inner courtyard still remains of a new house built by Sir John Giffard, d1556, but most of the present outer facades and state rooms are of campaigns in the early and late 18th century, the saloon corresponding to the original great hall.

COPPENHALL GORSE SJ 906203

The large overgrown platform is now again surrounded by water which is of considerable width on the SE side. Excavation of the platform in 1951 found evidence of occupation of the site in the 14th century.

DUDLEY CASTLE SO 946907 O

William the Conqueror gave extensive estates centred on Dudley to William Fitz-Ansculf c1071. The Domesday survey of 1086 states that "the said William holds Dudley and there is his castle", so the earthworks evidently existed by then. Early in the 12th century a large part of Fitz-Ansculf's estates, including Dudley, passed to Fulk Paganel, probably by marriage. Fulk's son Ralph supported the Empress Matilda against King Stephen. In 1130 the king came to Dudley and laid waste the district, although the castle appears to have remained untaken. In 1175 it was destroyed by Henry II as a consequence of Ralph's son Gervase having supported the king's sons in their rebellion of 1174. Gervase later paid 500 marks to regain his lands and the king's favour,, and at his death in 1194 was succeeded by his sister's son Ralph de Somery. At that time the site was either unused or only ranked as an unfortified house despite the formidable surrounding earthworks.

Roger de Somery began to refortify his manor house at Dudley but Henry III prevented the work from proceeding until 1264, when, having gained royal favour after supporting the king against the rebel barons, he was licensed to make the manor house into a castle with a ditch and a wall of stone and lime. The bailey wall may thus have been constructed by him or his son Roger, who succeeded in 1282, but it is fairly certain that the keep on the mound was erected during the troubled reign of Edward II by John de Somery. He succeeded as a minor in 1291, was knighted in 1306, and died childless in 1321. William de Beresford and other neighbours complained of John "that he has obtained such mastery in the county of Stafford that no man can obtain law or justice therein; that he has made himself more than a king there; that no-one can dwell there unless he buys protection from him either by money or assisting him in building his castles, and that he attacks people in their own houses with the intention of killing them unless they make fine for his protection".

On John de Somery's death Dudley went to his sister Margaret, wife of John de Sutton. The latter became heavily in debt to John de Charlton. Probably on the strength of the debt de Charlton was in possession of Dudley in 1329-30 when it was besieged by a number of local notables, although the full circumstances and outcome of the incident are not known. The Sutton fortunes must have recovered for in the 1340s and 50s they erected at Dudley a new hall and a block containing the principal private apartments and a chapel.

Old print of Dudley Castle

The keep, Dudley Castle

Interior of keep at Dudley Castle

The sixth successive John de Sutton served Henry VI as Lord Lieutenant of Ireland. He was wounded at the battle of St Albans inn 1455 and was later briefly incarcerated by Edward IV in the Tower of London. By the time of his death in 1487, aged about 86, the family had mostly dropped the Sutton surname in favour of that of Dudley. John's grandson Edmund Dudley did much to build up Henry VII's fortune. Vastly unpopular, he was ungratefully executed in 1510 by the heir who spent the fortune, Henry VIII. Edmund's son John, however, rose high in the royal favour, being created Viscount Lisle in 1542, Earl of Warwick in 1547, and becoming Duke of Northumberland under Edward VI. This John obtained Dudley in the 1530s after his cousin Edward, Lord Dudley, eighth in the Sutton line, surrendered his interest in the castle to a group of courtiers. John rebuilt the hall, providing a fine new set of apartments beyond it. The outer bailey walls also appear to be mostly of his time. Queen Mary executed him in 1553 after his abortive attempt to crown as Queen the Lady Jane Grey, married to his youngest son Lord Guildford Dudley. In 1554 Dudley Castle was granted to his kinsman Edward Dudley and in 1575 he entertained Queen Elizabeth at the castle. In the 1580s the castle was surveyed as a possible place of confinement for Mary, Queen of Scots, but in the end was never used as such.

On the death of the last of the Sutton Dudleys in 1643 the castle passed to the Ward family. It was held for King Charles in 1643 by Thomas Leveson, and in 1644 withstood a siege by the Earl of Denbigh until a relief force arrived from Worcester. It was eventually surrendered without a siege in 1646 to Sir William Brereton and in 12647 was made untenable by demolishing the outer parts of the keep and barbican and breaching the bailey walls. The domestic buildings remained in use and in the 1690s Edward Ward, Lord Dudley built a new block of apartments between the keep and gatehouse. The Ward family only finally transferred to Himley Hall after the apartments at Dudley were accidentally destroyed by a fire in 1750.

Dudley Castle lies 200m up on a limestone ridge high above the town. It has an oval bailey 100m long from north to south by 80m wide with a mound rising a further 9m in the SW corner. The surrounding ditch on the north side now contains pools for sea-lions, as the surrounding grounds have become a zoo, and beyond it is an outer platform. Another outer platform on the south has this 16th century outer walls with a modest round corner tower and a rectangular gatehouse.

The main courtyard is surrounded by a curtain wall 2m thick. On the SE the curtain is thought to be 12th century, but most of the rest is of c1270-1320, but with much rebuilding and patching later. The wall has been heightened on the east side where the domestic apartments lie against it. On the north side it has been replaced by thinner 16th century walling with an unfortified secondary gateway. Considerable parts of the western walls were destroyed in 1647. The square gatehouse on the south side incorporates 12th century masonry in the side walls flanking the vaulted passage. The early 14th century inner and outer gateway arches have portcullis grooves. In front of the outer arch is a mid to late 14th century barbican taking the form of an open porch with two round corner towers, the outer parts of which were destroyed in 1647. The outer arch of the barbican, linking the remains of the towers, is a 16th century insertion. West of the gateway is a block of the 1690s recently re-reroofed to provide a cafe and toilets.

The ruined hall on the east side was a splendid chamber nearly 24m long by 9.5m wide above cellars. It was built under the direction of Sir William Sharington for the Earl of Northumberland c1550. A central set of steps led up to a loggia on the west side. At the south end of the loggia was a staircase and at the north end was a porch giving onto the service end of the hall, probably screened off with a musicians gallery above the service passage. North of the hall are a pair of 16th century ranges, the nearest having a bow window, and the furthest an octagonal stair turret near the north gateway. Both ranges contained service rooms at courtyard level, two storeys of fine apartments above with large windows towards the court, and there were attics in the gabled roofs above. South of the hall is a large mid 14th century block with the solar and chapel set side by side over cellars. The chapel has a fine ogival headed window on the south side.

Outer ward at Dudley Castle

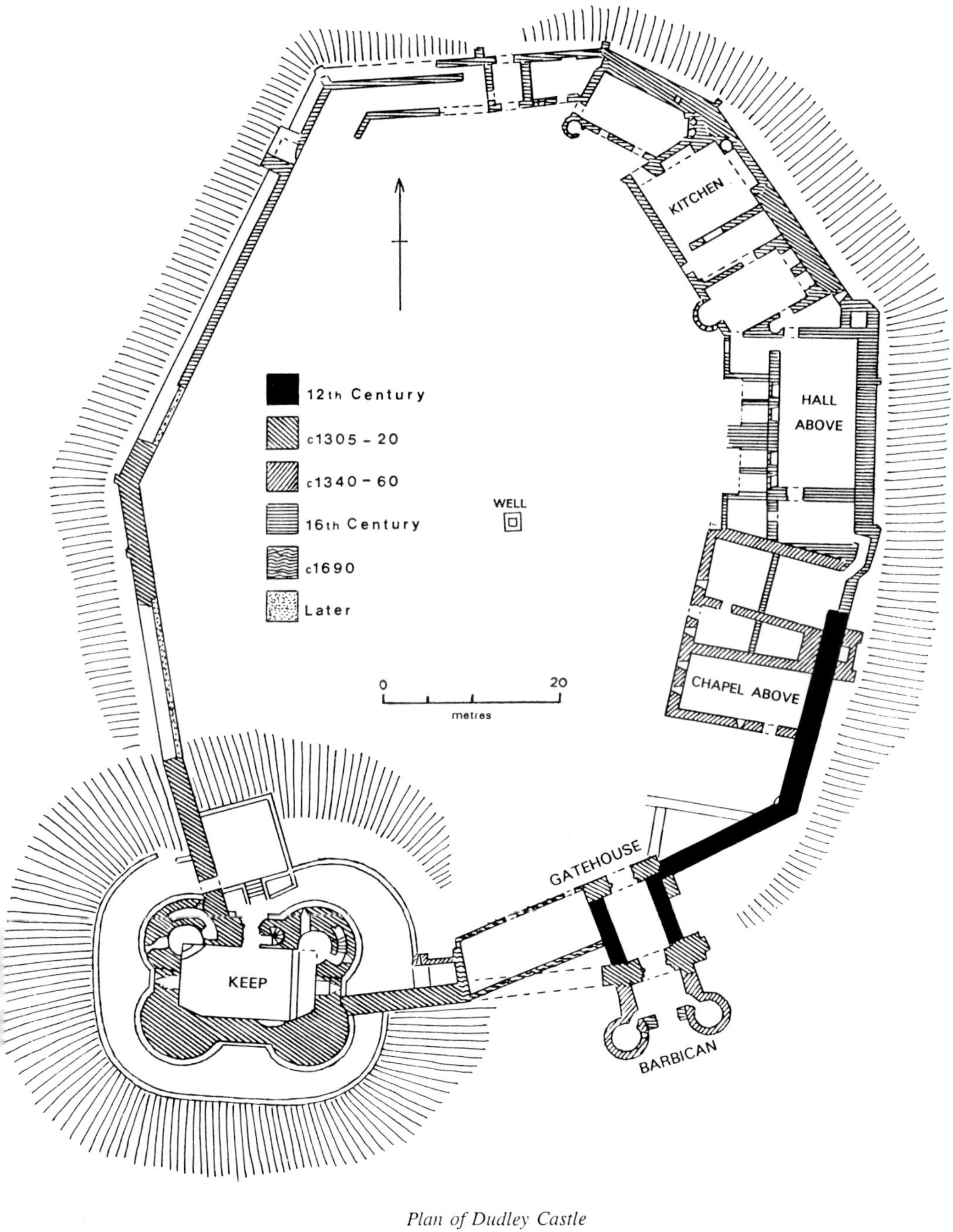

Plan of Dudley Castle

The keep at Dudley Castle

Interior of keep at Dudley Castle

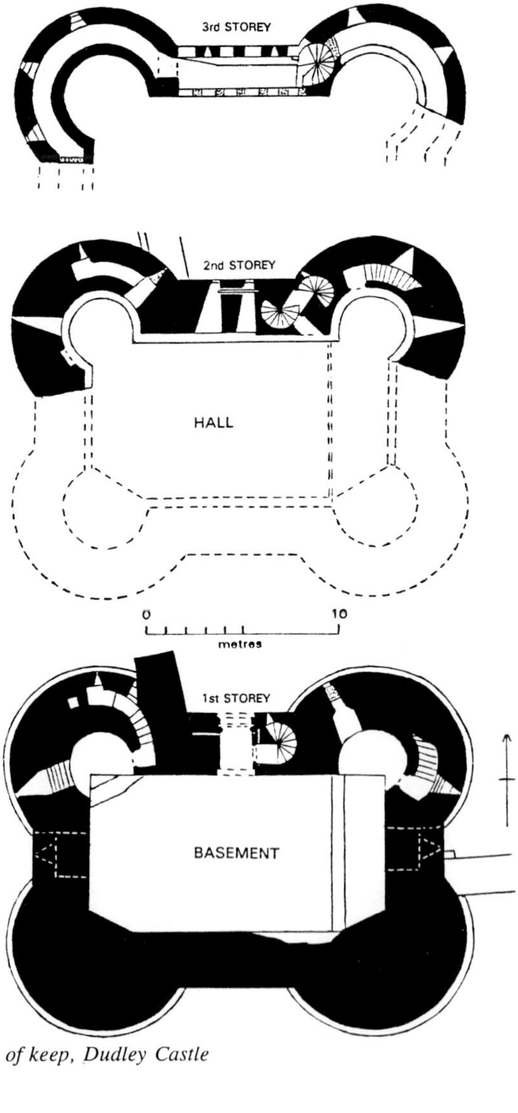

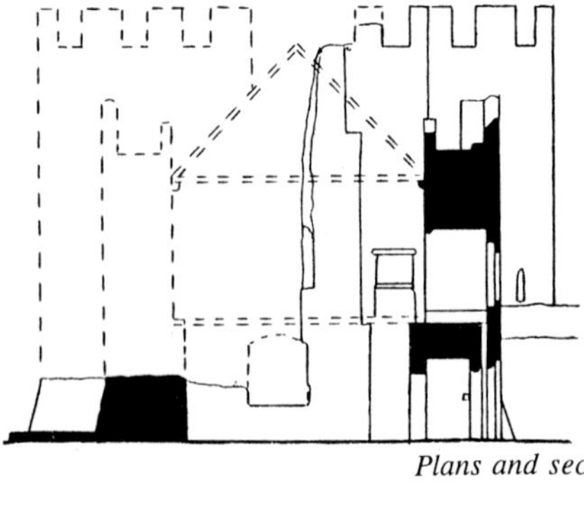

Plans and section of keep, Dudley Castle

Old print of the domestic buildings at Dudley Castle

The summit of the mound had a low chemise or parapet surrounding the keep and was originally reached from the summit of the south curtain by means of a drawbridge over a pit leading to a gateway in a small turret. In the 16th century the part of the chemise facing the bailey was rebuilt and a kitchen provided on the north, beside the west curtain wall. The keep is still imposing and of great interest despite the southern or outermost part of it having been destroyed to within 2m of the mound summit level in 1647. The keep is 21.8m long by 14.8m wide externally and has a circular tower 9.8m in external diameter projecting slightly from each corner. At the lowest level the southern towers were solid and the main walls are 3m thick, except for the thicker north wall containing the entrance. This was closed by a portcullis operated from two narrow embrasures with windows lighting the main room above. From the eastern side of the entrance rises a spiral stair up to the east end of the main room, which seems to have been screened off beyond it, i.e. the stair opened into the room, not the service passage. At this upper level the NE tower contained a service room with a secondary stair for servants to use to bring up food and drink. The NW tower contains a fireplace and a latrine and may have been partitioned off, although it would have been rather dark and small to have been the lord's bedroom. Indeed the keep was probably used for ceremonial purposes, as a means to overawe the neighbours, and as a refuge. It is doubtful whether the lord would normally sleep within the keep although it is possible that a more comfortable sleeping space was available in the SW tower. From the top of the main stair a secondary spiral stair leads to the wall-walk 11m above the motte summit. The towers contained galleries in their outer walls at this level to allow access to the other sections of wall-walk. The towers appear to have been roofed over at the same level as the main roof, without habitable spaces above, but their walls rose one more level to higher battlements with merlons reaching 16m above the ground. The upper fighting levels on the towers were either unusable dummies or had wooden platforms reached by ladders. Clearly the real reason why the towers rose one more level was to make a much more impressive building to display Sir John Somery's might and wealth.

DUNSTALL HALL SJ 902002

A new housing estate lies upon the site of the Courtaulds factory, for the construction of which earlier in the 20th century the hall and its moat and gatehouse were obliterated. Dunstall was owned by the Hampton family until the late 15th century, and the hall is likely to have been rebuilt by Humphrey Moseley after he purchased it in 1566. The estate was later purchased in turn by the Wightwick family, the Hoskinsons, and then in 1793 by James Hordern, by whom the house was repaired and the moat preserved.

ECCLESHALL CASTLE SJ 828296 O

Eccleshall belonged to the Bishops of Coventry and Lichfield from an early period. In 1200 Bishop Muschamp was licensed by King John to fortify his manor house set on flat ground beside a stream to the north of the church. The enclosure of that period is thought to have been semi-circular in shape. The present rectangular court was laid out by Walter Langton, bishop from 1297 to 1321. He was Treasurer of England under Edward I but was imprisoned by Edward II, although later restored to office. Of his work there remains a three storey polygonal tower at the NE corner, the lower part of the 2m thick curtain wall on the north, east, and southern sides, the east and south arms of the moat, long since drained, and perhaps the stone bridge with four breakwater buttresses crossing the moat on the south side. Originally there were probably towers on the other corners and on either side of a gateway in the south wall. It is likely that the original hall and other apartments lay on the north side of the court, which was about 75m long from east to west by 54m wide.

In 1642 Bishop Wright garrisoned the castle for Charles I. He died within it in 1643 while under siege from a Parliamentary force which occupied the nearby parish church which has a high west tower commanding the castle. A Royalist force arrived to relieve the castle and was on the point of taking away the Bishop's body and a quantity of treasure from the castle when a troop of Parliamentary horse arrived from Stafford. The Royalists fled in confusion leaving only ten men in the castle who were forced to yield soon afterwards when the gatehouse was captured in a night assault. In 1646 Parliament ordered the castle defences dismantled but the bishops continued to use it as a residence and in the 1690s Bishop Lloyd erected the present house on the west side of the court. It has a thirteen bay east facade and two shallow wings and there are later outbuildings to the east and north.

Eccleshall Castle

FINCHFIELD MOAT SO 883971

The house platform and the damp depressions which were relics of the three arms of the surrounding wet moat 2m deep were excavated in 1983 prior to being built upon, but nothing of interest was found.

HAMSTALL HALL SK 105194

Hardly any traces now remain of the mansion of the de Ridware family by the west bank of the River Blythe south of the bridge. A comparatively small but imposing brick tower immediately north of the churchyard was the status symbol and lookout tower of a quadrangular mansion built by the Coton family c1500. Later in the 16th century the Fitzherberts enlarged the hall and the tower was then adapted to serve as a stair turret. Most of the mansion was demolished in the 18th century and its assumed moat has vanished but the tower was allowed to remain in a derelict state as a folly or eye-catcher visible from a new house. A brick gatehouse with a pair of low octagonal turrets remains to the north.

Lookout tower at Hamstall Ridware

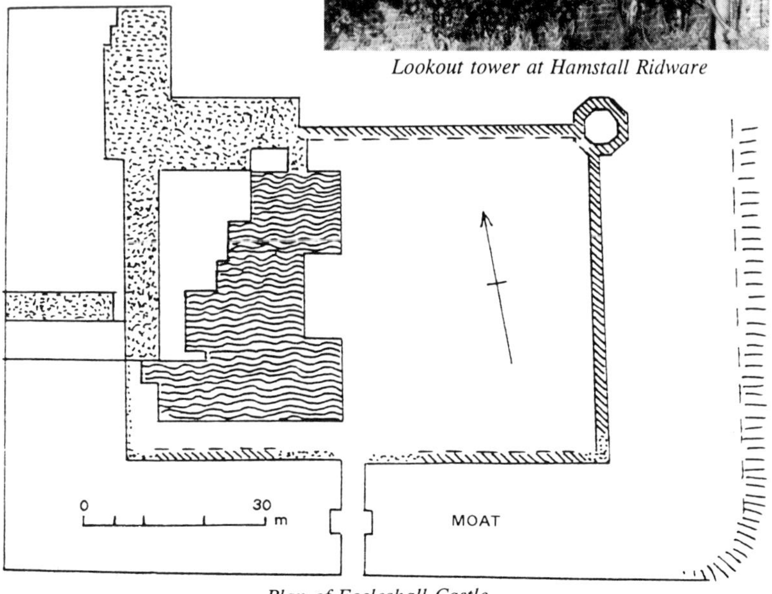

Plan of Eccleshall Castle

HANDSACRE HALL SK 090156

Three dry arms of the moat survive beside a new housing estate. A drawbridge remained until the early 18th century. In his book of 1798 Stebbing Shaw reported that the derelict timber mansion then standing within the moat contained a beam dated 1663, no doubt recalled a rebuilding or repair.

HAUGHTON MOTTE SJ 865204

There are slight remains of an earthwork to the west of the parish church which may have been a small motte.

HEIGHLEY CASTLE SJ 773467

Heighley Castle is spectacularly placed on a high wooded hill north of Madeley. It has an irregularly shaped courtyard over 100m long with a maximum width of 50m, with very steep falls to the east and south and a deep ditch separating it from the rest of the hill on the other two sides. Stone from cutting the ditch was used to build a thick curtain wall on the inner side but only buried footings now remain of it. Overlooking a causeway across the ditch at the NW corner is a standing fragment of corework and foundations suggesting the presence here of a D-shaped tower about 12m across. It is likely that there was once a second such tower with the gateway between them. The bailey slopes markedly down towards the south end where there appears to have been a suite of apartments. The exposed arcaded wall running from east to west formed the north wall of a vaulted undercroft of late 13th or 14th century date. There must have been an important chamber above, probably the solar. This would accord with the first certain mention of the castle itself in 1276, but the defences are assumed to have been built in the 1220s by Henry de Audley in imitation of the Earl of Chester's castle at Beeston in Cheshire which has a very similar position. Certainly in 1223 de Audley was given a dozen hinds from the royal forest of Cannock to stock his park here. Early 14th century estimates of the value of the castle suggest it was then in a neglected state but it appears to have been sufficiently in repair for it to be used as a prison in 1534, and to warrant demolition in the Civil War to prevent it being occupied by Royalists.

Heighley Castle

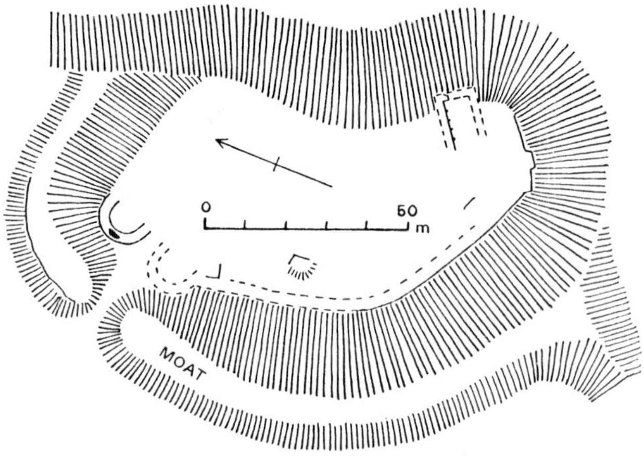

Plan of Heighley Castle

The old hall at Himley in 1735

HIMLEY HALL SO 888916

The present 18th century hall with extensions of 1824-7 built by the Ward family lies on or close to the site of a late medieval moated mansion of brick and stone shown still intact in an engraving of 1735 published in Shaw's book in 1798. The wet moat may have dated back to the time of William Beresford, owner c1316 under the overlordship of John de Somery of Dudley, but the picture suggests that much of the house as it stood in 1735 was erected in the 15th and 16th centuries. By 1346 the manor had passed to John, son of Margaret de Sutton, and his widow Isabel probably lived here until she died in 1397. It then reverted to the lords of Dudley. It is likely that much of the house standing in 1735 was built by Sir John Dudley, who acquired the estate in 1537 and later became Duke of Northumberland (see page 23)

Undercroft of probable solar at Heighley Castle

LAPLEY MANOR SJ 873130

There are slight remains of the ditch which surrounded the precinct of Lapley Priory. After it was dissolved as an alien priory by Henry V in the early 15th century a manor house was built on the elevated site of the former convent buildings to the north of the church. The position was walled and probably moated, and in 1643 held a Parliamentary garrison of 70 men. In December of that year Colonel Heveningham captured the house for King Charles by scaling the walls with ladders. Most of the enclosing wall was demolished soon afterwards and it does not appear on as drawing of the house made c1800 although parts then still survived.

LICHFIELD CASTLE AND CATHEDRAL CLOSE SK116097 F

A castle built at Lichfield in 1129 probably stood in the area of Ware Street and Frog Street. It was destroyed under the terms of a treaty of 1148 between the Earl of Chester and the Earl of Leicester. When Leland visited Lichfield c1540 the name Castle Field was still in use and he comments on there having been a "castle of anciente tyme in the south part of the town, but no part of it standeth". The town seems to have once had a boundary ditch but Leland is adamant that "there is no token that ever the town was waullyd".

The rectangular close about 270m long by 190m wide surrounding the cathedral is divided from the town on the south side by the Minster Pool. On the other sides was a dry ditch 30m wide and 5m deep, still remaining in an overgrown state on the north and east. The ditch was probably first cut c1130 by Bishop Roger de Clinton, but if so is likely to have been widened in 1299, when under the terms of a licence granted by Edward I to Bishop Walter Langton, the close was surrounded by an embattled wall with gateways on the west and SE. Langton built himself a palace against the east wall in the NE corner of the close in 1304-14 but nothing remains of it. The palace was a purely domestic building relying on the close wall for security.

Foundations of gatehouse tower at Lichfield Cathedral Close

Parts of the north and east walls of the close survive with a polygonal turret attached to a contemporary square building (St Mary's House) in the SE corner, and the lower part of a polygonal tower at the NE corner with a vaulted basement and much later patching in brick. Nothing survives of intermediate towers on the east side or of the the other corner towers, their ruins being removed after the Civil War. The NW tower bore a statue of Bishop Langton. Excavations a few years ago revealed the base of the eastern of a pair of polygonal towers flanking the south gate. This gateway was demolished in the mid 18th century to allow better access for coaches. Most of the west gate was demolished in 1800 to make room for Newton's College. It was completed by Bishop Newburgh, who succeeded Bishop Langton in 1322, and was an oblong block adorned with coats of arms, and by 1530 it also had a statue of the Virgin Mary.

The close was garrisoned for King Charles in 1642. In March 1643 Lord Brooke was fatally wounded whilst leading an attack on the west gate,. Sir John Gell continued the attack with a bombardment from the south and the garrison yielded two days later. Prince Rupert recaptured the close after a ten day siege a few weeks later and King Charles visited it three times in 1645. Sir William Brereton besieged the close from April 1646 until mid-July, when under agreed terms of surrender the garrison of 700 men with 85 officers and other refugees were allowed to leave. During the siege the cathedral central spire was brought down by cannon fire. In 1649 the close, cathedral, the bishop's palace in the NE corner and many of the other buildings all lay in ruins. A new bishop's palace, on the same site, but differently aligned, erected in 1687-8, now serves as a school. Much of the external stonework of the cathedral is 18th century and later.

SE corner tower of Lichfield Cathedral Close

LITTYWOOD MOAT SJ 889190

The evocative surname de la Motte is associated with this site in 1175 and suggests that the earthworks are at least partly of that period. The innermost of two concentric circular moats is certainly earlier than the centrally placed timber hall with brick infilling which was erected c1400 for the de Caverswall family. The wide inner moat is dry but for a small pool, and surrounds a platform roughly 35m square. The outer moat is about one fifth water filled and encloses an area about 160m in diameter.

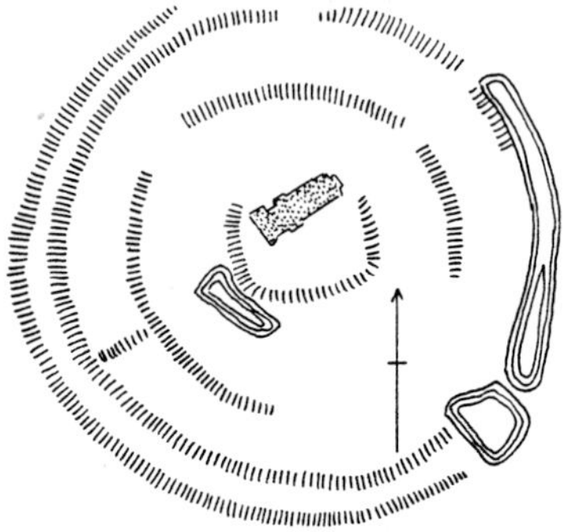

Plan of Littywood Moat

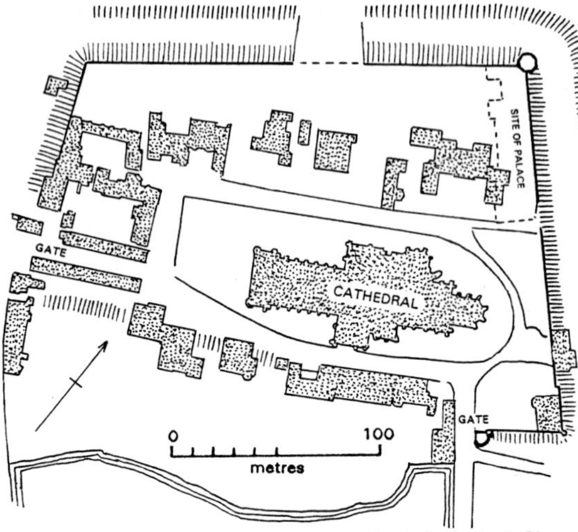

Plan of Lichfield Cathedral Close

MADELEY MANOR HOUSE SJ 773423 V

Ralph, Lord Stafford was licensed to crenellate his manor house at Madeley in 1348, and what remains is likely to be of that period. The site is flat and boggy, beside a stream south of Madeley village. A wet moat enclosed a rectangular platform measuring 80m from north to south by 67m from east to west. The east and south arms of the moat are now only represented by shallow depressions, but the other two arms still contain over 12m width of water. Beyond them is a narrow outer wet moat to the west and a ditch containing the stream on the north so originally there may have been a complete double circuit of wet moats. There are further outworks to the west. A walled court and house occupied the NE corner of the platform. All that remains of them is a length of the 1.7m thick west wall of the court with the southern jamb of a gateway with a portcullis groove.

Madeley Manor House

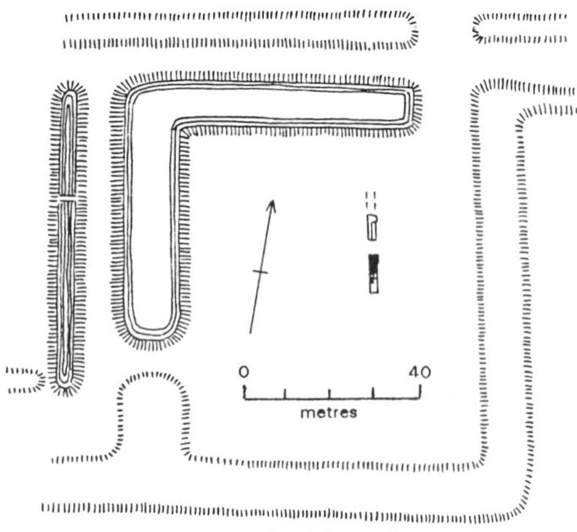

Plan of Madeley Manor House

Madeley Manor House

MAVESYN RIDWARE HALL SK 081168 V

Nothing remains of the moat which once surrounded the mansion. The gatehouse range of a quadrangular building set around a courtyard still survives in front of a house of 1718. The range is 14th century and is timber framed except for the outer wall, which is of stone with a brick superstructure probably of 1718. The house was built by the Mavesyn family but after Sir Robert Mavesyn was killed at the battle of Shrewsbury in 1403 it passed to the Cawarden family. Monuments of both families lie in the church.

MOAT HOUSE, TAMWORTH SK 202039

Lying off Lichfield Street, west of the castle, is a brick mansion with a symmetrical design with slightly projecting wings, said to have been built in the 1570s by the Comberford family. It has traces of its former moat filled with water from the adjacent River Teme. The Venetian window in a wing is a later insertion.

Gatehouse range at Mavesyn Ridware Hall

NEWCASTLE-UNDER-LYME CASTLE SJ 844459

The date and circumstances of the founding of this building are not known. It may have been built by Henry I in the early 12th century and named Newcastle as being a substitute for the former royal castle at Stafford, with the appendage "under Lyme" from the tract of forest of that name in the adjacent part of Cheshire. Alternatively it may have been built by Ralph Gernons, Earl of Cheshire, being one of several castles which he was forced to have surrendered to King Stephen after being captured at Northampton in 1146. Newcastle was restored to the earl in 1149 and he was confirmed in his extensive estates at Henry II's accession in 1154, although the king took the castle back and retained it after the Earl was murdered by William Peveril later in that year.

There are many records of expenditure by Henry II, Richard I, and John on maintenance to the defences and buildings and the keeping of garrisons at Newcastle. The large sum of £37 spent on the castle pool in 1171 suggests that the water defences were then being created or substantially improved. There was a rectangular stone tower keep and probably other stone buildings there by 1192. At that time the garrison numbered 5 knights, 15 mounted serjeants, and 30 foot-serjeants. A body of 180 footmen were hired to strengthen the garrison in 1195-6. King John spent over £200 on the castle, visited it in 1206, and in 1215 granted it to the Earl of Chester. On the Earl's death in 1232 Henry III recovered the castle. It was held from then until 1234 by Gilbert de Segrave, whilst Henry de Audley became keeper in 1238. In 1264 Henry III granted the castle to his captor Simon de Montfort, but the latter was defeated and killed at the battle of Evesham in 1265 and in 1267 Newcastle was given by Henry III to his younger son Edmund, thus establishing the connection between Newcastle and the Duchy of Lancaster which lasted until the 20th century. John of Gaunt, Duke of Lancaster had repairs made to Newcastle in the 1370s and the duchy accounts suggest it was well maintained until the 1440s after which Henry VI neglected it in favour of Tutbury, although minor repairs were carried out in 1478-9. Leland c1541 says that "All the castel is doune save one great toure" so its demise must have been quite rapid. The buildings were "altogether decayed" by 1610 when leased to the Sneyd family. In 1828 they purchased the site from the Duchy and drained the marshy land which had formerly been the castle pool.

Over a century and half ago there was still extant a book of Chaucer's poems published in 1602 into which a few years later had been written a description of the castle. "......New Castle was no more nor 150 paces from south to north, but well nigh two hundred from est to west; and had two transepts and four bays with dungen tower of twenty paces square, which rose in three storeys of full height of seventy feet.....a low portal, and not well lighted passage did admit to the hall, very large and spacious, with roof loftie, and painted with devices, galleries for the minstralls, and the walls clothed with geer of warfare.....wending a gloomy staircase did lead to the state rooms and bedd-chamber of the Prince, and other on the upper for the companie.....The walls outer had good buttresses to the height of thirty feet and the whole was moer fytt as a statelie confortable dwellinge then as a fortress of defence, cause of the rising landes south and este....."

All that now remains of the castle is part of the much reduced mound beside a bowling green in Silverdale Road. The bailey site, now covered with housing, was to the north, while the other three sides were protected by a lake created by damming up the Lyme Brook. This area is now covered by a thick layer of silt. Excavations have revealed the foundations of a long narrow building SW of the mound, and on the north side was found a long wall with a chamfered plinth and buttresses.

Last remains of Norbury Manor

NORBURY MANOR SJ 797233 V

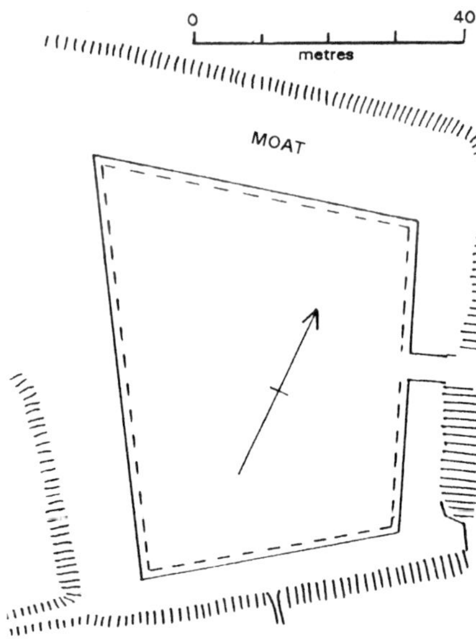

Plan of Norbury Manor

According to Stebbing Shaw the moated mansion at Norbury was built by Ralph Butler the elder, lord of Norbury from c1291 to 1307. In 1521 the Butlers sold the manor to Thomas Skrymsher, d1551, a prothonotary of the Court of Common Pleas. The Shrymshers in turn sold Norbury to George Anson of Shugborough in 1775. By 1801 the manor house was in a state of decay and was only inhabited by farmworkers. It was demolished in 1838 and a new farmhouse built some way to the south. Although the old house is thus lost its platform still remains, being an irregularly shaped quadrangle with sides about 64m, 38m, 47m and 48m long respectively, having ashlar faced retaining walls about a metre thick. The moat is now nearly dry. It was of variable width and widened into a pool at the west corner where a stream flows in.

Fortunately a drawing survives of the house as it was c1686. It shows the entrance front which faced NE. The gateway was positioned in the middle and appears to have then been reached by a bridge, although there is now a causeway in this position.The lower part of the walling with narrow window loops could well have been of c1300, but the round bartizan on bold corbelling at the east corner was probably somewhat later, while the upper two levels of mullioned and transomed windows with gables above to the south of the gateway, and the jettied single upper storey to the north, must have all been 16th century work.

Norbury Manor as it was c1686

OKEOVER HALL SK 158482

The moat shown around the house in Plot's view of 1686 could have dated back as far as the time of the Sir Hugh de Okeover who flourished c1180-1212. The Cockayne brothers of Ashbourne raided Okeover Hall in 1449 while Philip de Okeover was away in London. They seriously damaged the house and killed all but five of the deer in the surrounding park. The moat was probably filled in when Leak Okeover began rebuilding the then mostly 16th or 17th century house in 1745.

Pillaton Hall

PILLATON OLD HALL SJ 943129

The manor of Pillaton was held by Burton Abbey until it was dissolved, and then in 1546 was granted to Sir William Paget, whose descendants held it until the 18th century. However Pillaton Hall, SE of Penkridge, was occupied by the Littleton family from at least the early 16th century, if not earlier, and the chapel is probably late 15th century. In 1754 the moated house was taxed on no less than 25 hearths, a very considerable establishment, and was inhabited by Lady Littleton. A few years afterwards Sir Edward Littleton, 1st Lord Hatherton, moved further north to Teddesley, away from the mining between here and Cannock. In 1786 only a farmer lived in the hall and the chapel was ruinous. Demolition then described as imminent had taken place by 1800 when a drawing shows only the north range and eight tall chimney stacks from the other ranges which for some reason had been left standing. Several of these stacks had fallen by 1841, when Buckley made some drawings of the house, and currently only two survive. In 1884-8 the north range was repaired by Lord Hatherton.

The narrow north range is of brick with a gateway with four centred arches and turrets, although the latter may date from 1706 when the upper parts were rebuilt. In the NE corner lies the stone chapel of St Modwena with typical 15th century windows, battlements and buttresses. The hall lay in the south range and the solar was on the east, with the kitchen in the west range. In the 1980s a new west range was constructed in the old style to augment the limited amount of accommodation available in the north range. The moat was drained c1860, but narrow ornamental pools have now been laid out along the north and east sides.

PRESTWOOD MOAT SJ 946018

Prestwood is a corruption of Priestwood and was held by the Dean and chapter of the college at Wolverhampton, who are assumed to have leased it out to others since in the late 13th century Henry, son of William de Essex made "a certain watery place in the wood of Prestwood" The old house, by then a farm, was burnt in 1612, and its successor was built to the west. Part of the moat remained until 1972.

RED MOOR MOAT SK 043117

This rectangular platform 100m long by 70m wide lying in woodland beside a stream is probably the place that Henry II visited in 1155 after acquiring a small Cistercian abbey whose occupants had moved to Warwickshire. Money was spent on the house here in 1157 and 1162. The surrounding ditch is now almost dry.

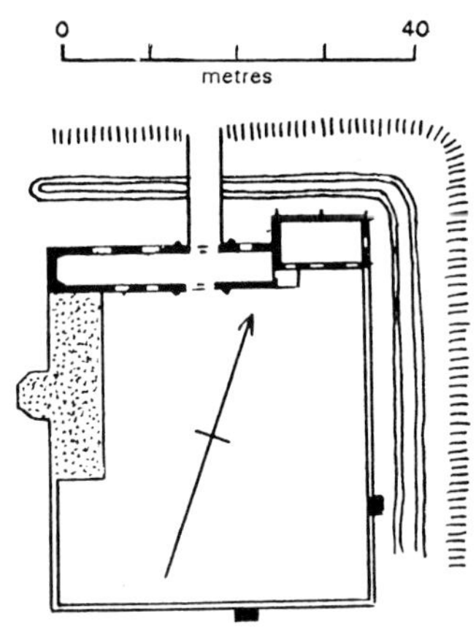

Plan of Pillaton Hall

RODBASTON HALL SJ 921124

The hereditary forester of Cannock had a castle in this area in 1154. It is mentioned as a manor house in 1199, but another record of 1215 calls it a castle. The remains appear to be relics of a moated and crenellated house built by John Saundersted in the 1330s. A moat with about 6m width of water encloses an overgrown tree-clad platform about 50m square. The linear mound 4m high on the SE side probably covers the debris and ruins of a stone domestic range. There is a gap in the moat, wider than it was formerly, towards the west end of the south side. The manor of Rodbaston was subsequently held by a series of different families but the moated house appears to have been occupied by the Eginton family as tenants from the 1380s until c1768.

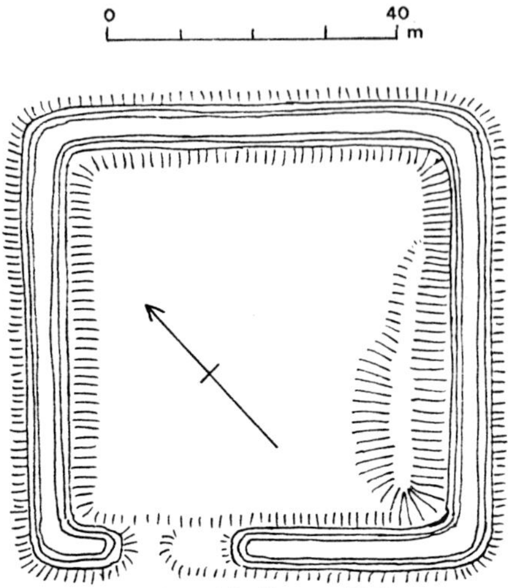

Plan of Rodbaston Hall

RUSHALL HALL SP 026998

Rushall formed part of the barony of Dudley until 1322 but from at least the 1160s was held by the Rushall family until the 1230s, when it passed to the Boweles family. The men working for William de Boweles whose tools were confiscated by officials of Cannock Forest in 1292 could have been illegally quarrying limestone for building the thin but high curtain wall at Rushall Hall. That it was needed is demonstrated by an incident in 1323 when a notorious local trouble-maker, John de Watales, attacked the house of William de Boweles at Rushall because he gave shelter to Robert de Eslinton. John was said to have shot arrows over the gate and was later fined. However the wall could be as late as c1400 when "Geffrey Ive pulled doun an olde hall at Rushale, and set up a newe hall" on the occasion of his daughter becoming the second wife of William Grobbere. About 30 years later their daughter brought Rushall by marriage to John Harpur. Later in the 15th century the Harpurs added the gatehouse on the western side of the court, whilst the Leighs, who obtained the manor in 1540, added a third storey to the gatehouse c1600.

Edward Leigh supported Parliament in the Civil War and in 1643 Rushall Hall was besieged and captured in his absence by a party of Royalists under Prince Rupert, Lady Leigh with "only helpe of her men and maides" having valiantly defended her house. In May 1644 the hall was besieged and captured by the Earl of Denbigh. He described it as "watered round about, admirable works where are four forts at each end of the house one, from the water to the top of the works is some four or five yards high, besides the breadth of the trench which is answerable to it, and a stone wall within the works much higher, besides a very strong drawbridge, and but only one passage through the stone wall into the house, which is as strong as art can make it, and within the wall, in the yard, they have made galleries for their better defence, and greate stones laid thick around the works, which upon any assault would have done as much execution as the muskets".

Doorway in SE tower, Stafford

Ralph, Lord Stafford, Hastings brass, Elsing, Norfolk.

Stafford Castle

The earthworks at Stafford Castle are extensive and impressive (see plan on page 5). The mound has a summit about 65m long from east to west by 40m wide although it was smaller in the Norman period. It was originally isolated from the D-shaped bailey to the NE by a ditch. The bailey measures over 100m across from the west to the sunken entrance on the east. It is known that the bailey contained throughout the medieval period a set of apartments, a kitchen, stables, a chapel of St Nicholas, barns and other storage and service buildings mostly constructed of timber. No evidence has been found of a stone curtain wall ever having been built to enclose the bailey and it presumably retained a palisade as late as the 15th century.

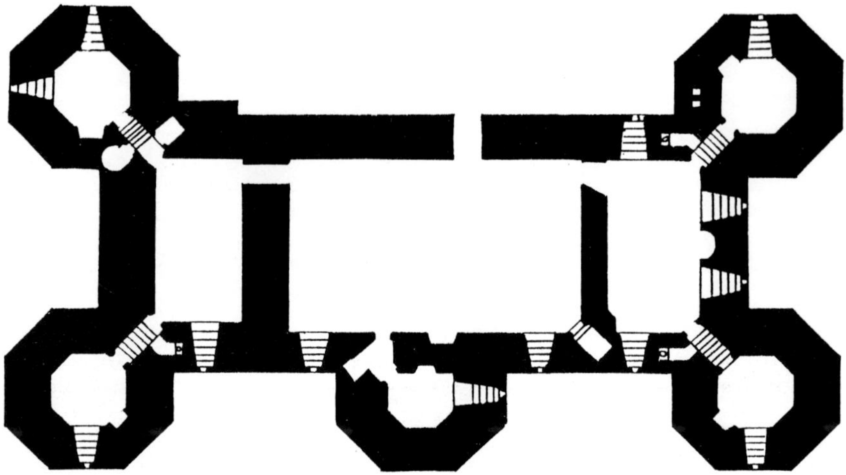

Plan of Stafford Castle in 1817

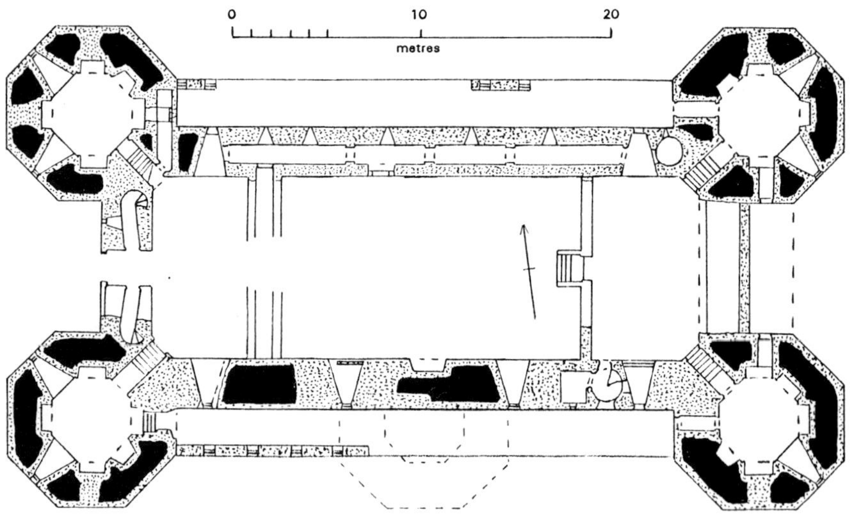

Plan of Stafford Castle in 1970

The excavations found evidence that in the Civil War the whole of the inner bailey was regarded as too large an area to defend with the available forces and that a part of it was divided off with earth and timber defences supplemented by gambions or wicker baskets filled with earth. To the east is an even larger outer bailey probably used only as a garden or for agricultural purposes in the late medieval period. Beyond it, extending nearly to St Mary's church, are traces of a settlement occupied from the 12th century until the 14th century.

Stafford Castle

In the 1960s what was then generally regarded as a dangerous 19th century ruin on the mound only escaped total demolition because of a suspicion that it might still incorporate 14th century work. The excavations begun in 1974 have indeed shown this to be true. It is now known that the mound originally had a smaller summit at a higher level that at present and in the 1340s this was shaved down to the internal size of the new stone building, the walls of which were built against it, giving a solid basement, except for a small wine cellar. The surplus earth was then piled up on the west end to lengthen the mound to support one end of a structure 24.4m long by 14.8m wide over walls which are rather thicker than the 7ft (2.1) stipulated in the contract of 1347. The west end appears to have been raised over the stump of a late 12th century tower keep presumably built against the original slope of the mound as at Guildford Castle.

The building on the mound had two main storeys, the lower being for servants and storage and the upper containing a central hall with a chamber at either end, that on the west being the solar. The octagonal corner towers 9m in diameter appear to have contained four storeys corresponding respectively to the solid base, the storage basement, the lord's suite, and the wall-walk on the main block. All the tower rooms except the topmost are recorded as having fireplaces. The plan made before the rebuilding shows a service stair in the walling of the NW tower, but there was uncertainty as to the position of the main entrance and the means of access up to the hall. These were presumably in the north wall, which had been almost destroyed by then, and in the rebuilding was provided with a passage linking the rooms. The contract of 1347 specified that the battlements were to be carried out from the walls with machicolation slots behind the parapet. When the 19th century restoration ground to a halt only the east end had been completed. The remainder only stood to its present height and was left open as a garden. The entrance at the west end replaced an original postern doorway.

The town of Stafford was protected by the River Sow on the west and south, and by streams and marshland on the other two sides. In 913 Ethelfleda surrounded the town with earth banks reinforced with timber. In the 1220s and 30s Henry III encouraged the rebuilding of the defences in stone. However, two early 17th century maps show that part of the NW side and nearly all of the west side of the town were then still. only protected by earth banks and palisades. This weakness may be how a body of carefully picked Parliamentary troopers were able to infiltrate and capture the town so easily in 1643. The maps show an opening on the west, rectangular gabled gatehouse without battlements on the south and east, and a more impressive gatehouse with twin round embattled towers on the north. The walls were ruinous by the 1670s. The North Gate was replaced by a house of correction late in the 17th century, the South Gate was demolished in 1777, and the East Gate was taken down c1800. However a fragment of its north wall survived and was moved to its present position by the ring-road in 1939. There are no other remains of the walls.

STOURTON CASTLE SO 859849

The royal forest of Kinver probably had a hunting lodge in this area by the reign of William II. A ditch was dug around the lodge in 1184-5 and the courtyard enclosed, presumably by a palisade, in the following year. Work was done on the King's chamber in 1187-8, and further work on the buildings in 1190-1. A fresh set of timber buildings on a new site at Stourton were erected in 1195-6. They included a hall and offices, a kitchen, a chamber, a gaol, and gate with a brattice, and were surrounded with a palisade 16ft high with a circumference of 16 perches. King John came here to hunt in 1207 and 1215. By 1222 the lodge was known as the castle of Kinver and John, son of Philip, the King's Forester for Kinver, fortified it with funds and timber provided by Henry III.

Sir John Vaux was made Keeper of Kinver Forest and Stourton Castle in 1310, and in 1316 was implicated in the murder in the castle of Sir Thomas Murdak. Vaux was acquitted, although he had subsequently married Sir Thomas's widow Gillian, who was sentenced to be burnt. In 1360 the Prior of Dudley was held at Stourton for an offence against the strict forest laws reserving all hunting for the king. In 1382 Richard de Hampton succeeded Hugh Tyrell as Lord of Kinver, and in 1391 his son John was licensed to have an oratory at Stourton Castle. His elder son, another John, was a courtier of Henry VI and held a number of important offices from the 1430s. It is likely that he improved the castle apartments. He was ejected from his offices and estates when Edward IV seized the throne in 1461, but he recovered Stourton for a short while in 1470 when Henry VI was briefly restored to power. He in 1472 and Edward IV gave Stourton to his own brother George, Duke of Clarence, by whom it was alienated to Tewkesbury Abbey, but it was later recovered by Henry VII.

Stourton Castle

Sir Reginald Pole and his wife Margaret, daughter of the late Duke of Clarence, are assumed to have been living at Stourton c1500 when their son Reginald was born. He was favoured by his relative Henry VIII, and was given various clerical offices. Later, however, he opposed Henry's divorce and retired to Rome, where he was created a cardinal and sent to persuade France and Spain to invade England. Pole survived attempts by King Henry's agents to murder him and returned as Archbishop of Canterbury when England was returned to allegiance to Rome under Queen Mary. With impeccable timing he died a few hours after her in 1558.

Old print of Stourton Castle

During the first two thirds of the 17th century Stourton Castle was occupied by the Whorwood family, who also had a second residence at Compton, NW of Kinver, until they sold it in 1650. John Whorwood appears to have remained neutral in the Civil War, but in 1644 the castle was taken by a Parliamentary force under Colonel Thomas Fox. It was surrendered back to the Royalists after Colonel Fox was routed on Stourbridge Heath by Sir Gilbert Gerard, Governor of Worcester. The defences were probably destroyed soon afterwards, and 18th century views show a many-gabled house standing on a flat platform with a buttressed retaining wall on the east and north sides, probably the lower part of the original 13th century curtain wall. The nearby mill was converted into a forge c1650 and the noise and vibration made Stourton Castle unsuitable as a residence for gentry. Throughout much of the 18th century it was occupied by a farming family called Hollins, whilst in the 19th century it was occupied by a succession of industrialists. The castle was sold in 1974 and remains occupied as a private residence.

Old print of Stourton Castle

Old print of Stourton Castle

Stourton Castle stands on an outcrop with the River Stour to the east and slopes to the north and south. The house stands on the site of a keep or small inner court, the space now being all roofed over. On the west side is a square 14th or 15th century tower similar to that at Holt in Worcestershire, although here externally disguised with rendering. The remaining ranges around the former open court are of brick and were built in the mid to late 16th century, although the gables are 17th century. The hall lay on the east side and had a porch tower which was demolished in the 1830s when Sir Robert Smirke was employed to oversee a series of very considerable alterations and additions, including the mock Jacobean wings projecting to the west. A walled court had been created on this side in the late 17th century. In 1832 the foundations of a pair of round towers belonging to and outer ward to the NW were discovered. These may have been part of the work authorised by Henry III in the 1220s.

SWYNNERTON CASTLE SJ 856347

Edward II licensed Roger de Swynnerton to crenellate his house here in 1315. A rectangular pool containing two small islands in the park south of the church marks the site. It is not known whether other defences apart from the moat were actually ever built. The present hall beside the church dates from the 1720s and was built for Thomas Fitzherbert.

TAMWORTH CASTLE SK 207039

King Offa, who ruled Mercia from 757 to 796, is said to have made Tamworth his capital, building a palace there and surrounding the town with a rampart and ditch. It remained the capital of Mercia until 874, when it was destroyed by the Danes and lay derelict for several decades. In 912 King Edward the Elder permitted his sister Ethelfleda to govern Mercia which by then had become a province within his kingdom. Excavations carried out at various times in the 20th century have established that the boundary of the medieval town originated with the earth and timber defences she had erected in 913. Her nephew Athelstan, King of England from 924 to 940, made Tamworth one of his seats, but the town was destroyed again in 943 by the Danes, and was never again a royal residence, although there was a royal mint in the town until the 12th century.

On the strength of this association with the Saxon kings the castle mound at Tamworth has been erroneously described in the past as of Saxon origin. However it is obviously a typical Norman artificial castle mound probably raised in the late 11th century by Robert Marmion. He is said to have held Tamworth and also the manor of Scrivelsby in Lincolnshire on condition of performing the office of Royal Champion, a hereditary post requiring the holder to come to coronations dressed and armed for combat and "oppose himself against any person who should gainsay the royal coronation". King John ordered the destruction of Tamworth Castle because Robert Marmion, 5th baron, sided with the barons against him at the time of Magna Carta, but this was evidently not carried out. The Marmion male line failed in 1294 and Edward I later granted the castle to Sir Alexander de Freville. He was Royal Champion at the coronation of Edward III in 1327. The King was then a minor and this is the only certain occasion when the role of Royal Champion was actually performed. The office was subsequently attached to the manor of Scrivelsby, which had passed to a younger daughter of the last male Marmion.

Tamworth Castle

In 1423 Tamworth Castle passed by marriage from the Frevilles to Sir Thomas Ferrers, son of the 5th Baron Ferrers of Groby in Leicestershire. His successors continued to use the keep as an occasional residence, and were carrying out repairs to it in 1541 when Leland visited the town. He records that the "base-court and great ward of the castle is cleane decayed and the wall fallen down, and therein be now but houses of office of noe notable building". The castle was visited three times by James I towards the end of his reign. On the second occasion he was accompanied by Prince Charles, who stayed at the Moat House to the west. The castle was garrisoned for King Charles in 1642 and was captured by Parliamentary forces in 1643. Somehow the keep managed to avoid being slighted.

In 1688 Ann Ferrers, heiress of Tamworth Castle, married Robert Shirley, heir of Baron Ferrers of Chartley, thus reuniting the two branches of the family. Their daughter and heiress in 1715 married James Crompton, 5th Earl of Northampton, and in 1751 another heiress brought the castle to George Townsend, created a Marquess in 1786. These families had residences elsewhere and rarely used the castle. In the 1790s the hall in the keep was leased to the industrialist Robert Peel for use as a forge in connection with the factory he had built nearby. In the Jubilee year of 1897 Tamworth Corporation purchased the castle from the Marquess Townsend. The former bailey was then laid out as a public garden with a bandstand, and the keep was renovated, opening in 1899 as the town museum, a function it still serves.

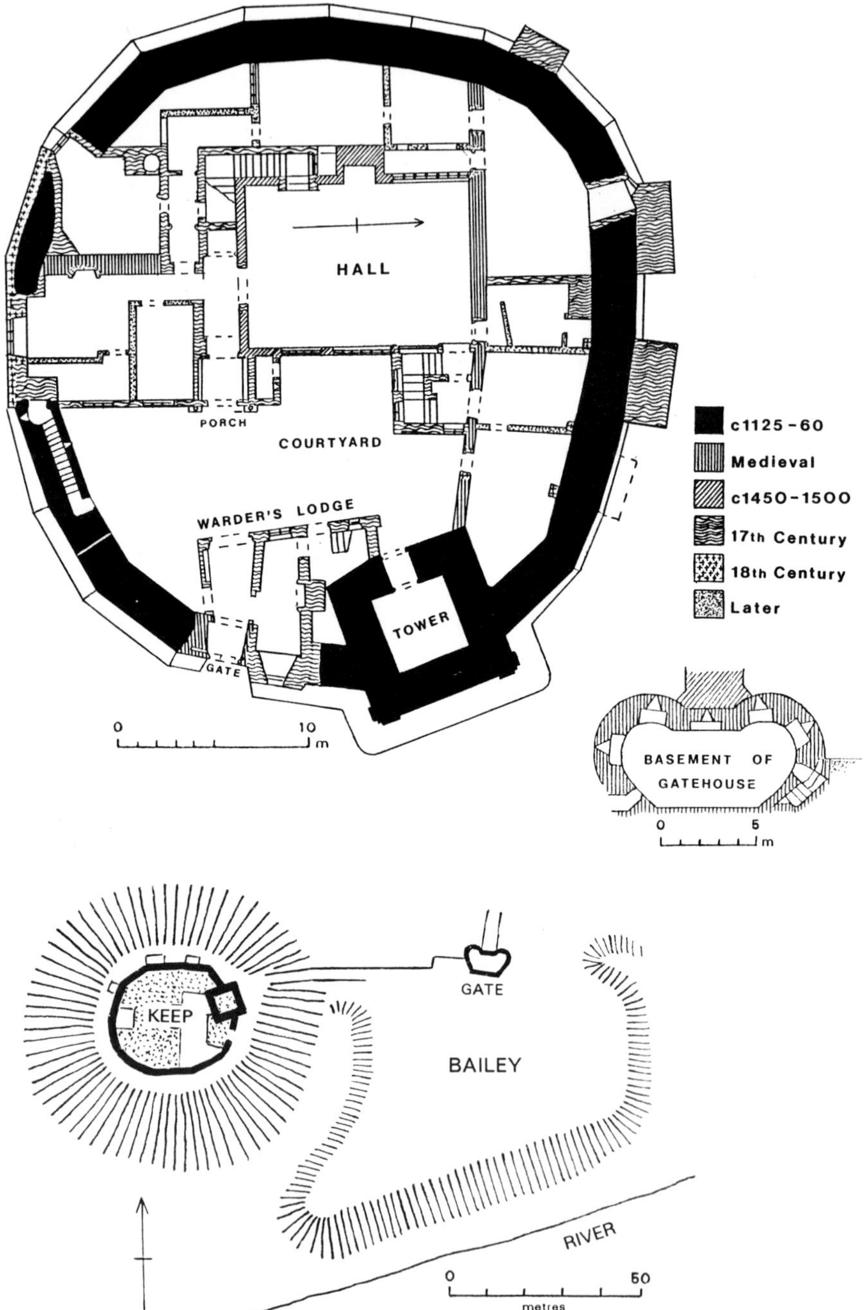

Plans of Tamworth Castle

Wall with herringbone masonry at Tamworth

Porch of domestic buildings, Tamworth Castle

The castle lies between the north bank of the River Tame and the main street of the town. As laid out in the late 11th century it comprised a large artificial mound standing in the NW corner of a quadrangular bailey about 90m long from east to west, with the east and west sides measuring about 35m and 60m long respectively. Excavations have revealed post holes of the original timber defences of the bailey. Nothing survives of any of the buildings within the bailey although an excavation near the bandstand revealed foundations of 16th century stables and outbuildings. In 1972-4 the interesting lowest storey of a gatehouse of c1260 on the north side close to the NE corner was revealed and left exposed. It has a sort of flattened heart shape with rounded parts flanking the entrance and is faced with fine ashlar. The surviving part, which contains several embrasures, was at moat level, the actual gate being above with at least one more storey above it. The gateway was originally approached by a timber bridge with a drawbridge at the inner end, but in the early 14th century the part of the bridge next the drawbridge was rebuilt in stone, and it was again rebuilt in the early 16th century. The upper parts of the gatehouse were demolished c1700 and the lower part incorporated in the cellars of the Town Hall Vaults public house removed c1970.

Crossing the motte ditch is a short but interesting section of curtain walling 2.7m thick, the walkway on top of which formed the only original access to the motte summit. This wall has extensive courses of herringbone masonry, a feature found in a number of Late Saxon and Early Norman churches but rarely in castles. Here is is unlikely to be earlier than c1100 or later than the 1140s.

The polygonal shell wall of coursed rubble with a high battered plinth without quoins is probably mid or late 12th centurya although it may be as late at the 13th century, which is undoubtedly the period of the entrance doorway. The shell wall has been later breached for the insertion of large bay windows but it is still one of the best preserved of its type in Britain. Above the plinth it is about 2.3m thick, and it rises 7.4m to a wall-walk protected by a parapet 3.8m high, although in its original form the wall was rather lower. The court within measures 31m from east to west by 28m from north to south. This is rather larger than many other shell keeps and has proved large enough to accommodate a dwelling considered adequate throughout later centuries, thus accounting for the preservation of this particular shell wall when so many others were already very decayed before the medieval period had ended.

Projecting slightly from the shell, commanding the approach, is a contemporary tower with walls 2m thick around an unlit basement about 4m square, although the walls are much thinner higher up. The outer corners of the tower have typical Norman pilaster buttresses slightly set back, and during a later remodelling round turrets have been added on these corners. The existing gateway arch beside the tower is later medieval in its present form and is surmounted by a Jacobean building called the Warder's Lodge. A window embrasure on the north side of the shell is thought to have been adapted from a former postern doorway.

Originally there would have been lean-to buildings around the inner face of the shell, with the hall perhaps where the kitchen and service buildings now are on the north. Walling in these ranges may be earlier than the late 15th century hall with its long axis set north to south and parallel to, but clear of, the west side. This leaves a narrow court between it and the gateway. The hall has been much remodelled, the entrance porch,, the staircases at the SW and NE corners, and much of the domestic apartments to the south being the work of Sir John Ferrers during James I's reign. Further alterations were carried out after the Civil War,,, and in the 18th century, including the projections beyond the outer face of the shell containing large windows.

Gatehouse interior at Tamworth Castle

Tamworth Castle

TRENTHAM CASTLE

A "castellum de Trentham" is mentioned in the Pipe Rolls for 1168. This may refer to a castle here also commemorated by the place name Mount Field, but it could also be an alternative name for the royal stronghold at Newcastle-under-Lyme.

Tamworth Castle

The South Tower, Tutbury

TUTBURY CASTLE SK 209291 O

The castle at Tutbury occupies a splendid defensive site above the River Dove that may have been utilised in Saxon times, but the existing motte with three baileys was erected in the 1070s. William I gave Tutbury to Hugh de Avranches but in 1071 it was transferred to Henry, Lord of Ferriers and Chambrais in Normandy, who thus became the first of the noble line known in England as the de Ferrers family. The castle appear to have been his principal residence in England and was the administration centre for the more than two hundred manors that he held. The town is mentioned in Domesday Book and retains part of its boundary rampart and ditch which are likely to be also of the 1070s or 80s.

Robert de Ferrers, third son of Henry, was created Earl of Derby in 1138. The castle was besieged and taken by Henry II in 1174 and destroyed soon afterwards as a consequence of William, 3rd Earl of Derby having joined the rebellion led by the king's sons. The chapel whose foundations lie in the middle of the court is assumed to have been built as part of a rebuilding of the castle in stone in the 1180s or 90s, and it is likely that the vanished shell keep on the mound was also of that period. Robert de Ferrers supported Simon de Montfort against Henry III and in 1263 Prince Edward laid waste his lands and did much damage to Tutbury Castle. After the rebel barons were defeated at Evesham in 1265 the earl lost his possessions and Tutbury was given by Henry III to his own younger son Edmund, created Earl of Lancaster in 1267. Edmund or his son Thomas built a new suite of apartments at the south end of the bailey, including a hall over 18m long, a great chamber 14m long, both being nearly 9m wide. They survived until at least the end of the 16th century. In 1313-4 Earl Thomas spent £100 on building the existing gatehouse. He led the baronial opposition to Edward II and was captured and executed in 1322 after being defeated at Burton. Tutbury Castle was plundered but most of the Earl's money was lost in the River Dove whilst being carted away and was not found until the 19th century.

In 1326 Edward II returned Tutbury to Thomas's brother Henry. His heiress Blanche married Edward III's third son John of Gaunt, then created Duke of Lancaster. John himself was often abroad, in London, or at one of his many other castles, but Tutbury seems to have been frequently used by his wife. Repairs are recorded in 1362, and some new walling in the 1390s. When John died in 1399 The Duchy of Lancaster was seized by he nephew Richard II and it has belonged to the sovereign ever since as in the same year the rightful heir to the Duchy, John's son Henry, returned from exile and deposed Richard and was himself crowned as Henry IV. A new tower, which has not survived, was being built at the time of King Henry's visits to Tutbury in 1404 and 1405, and work on a fresh section of curtain walling was begun prior to his death in 1413. Under his grandson Henry VI much of the present curtain wall around the bailey was built, the work being commenced at the southern end in 1420. It proceeded slowly until 1442, when the South Tower was begun. From 1446 until Edward IV seized the throne in 1461, Tutbury was held by the Queen, Margaret of Anjou. The South Tower was completed in the 1450s and the North Tower was under construction in 1457-60.

Despite all this new work the castle was approaching obsolescence as both a fortress and residence and subsequent monarchs had little use for it. The shell keep was ruined by the 1490s, the kitchen roof fell down by 1516, and by 1523 many roofs were leaking and a 30m long section of the curtain wall between the North Tower and the gatehouse was split lengthways from top to bottom. A survey in 1559 called the castle "indifferently" well repaired and the sketch of the castle made about that time is perhaps a fanciful view of what it had looked like a couple of generations earlier rather than what it actually looked like then.

The gatehouse at Tutbury

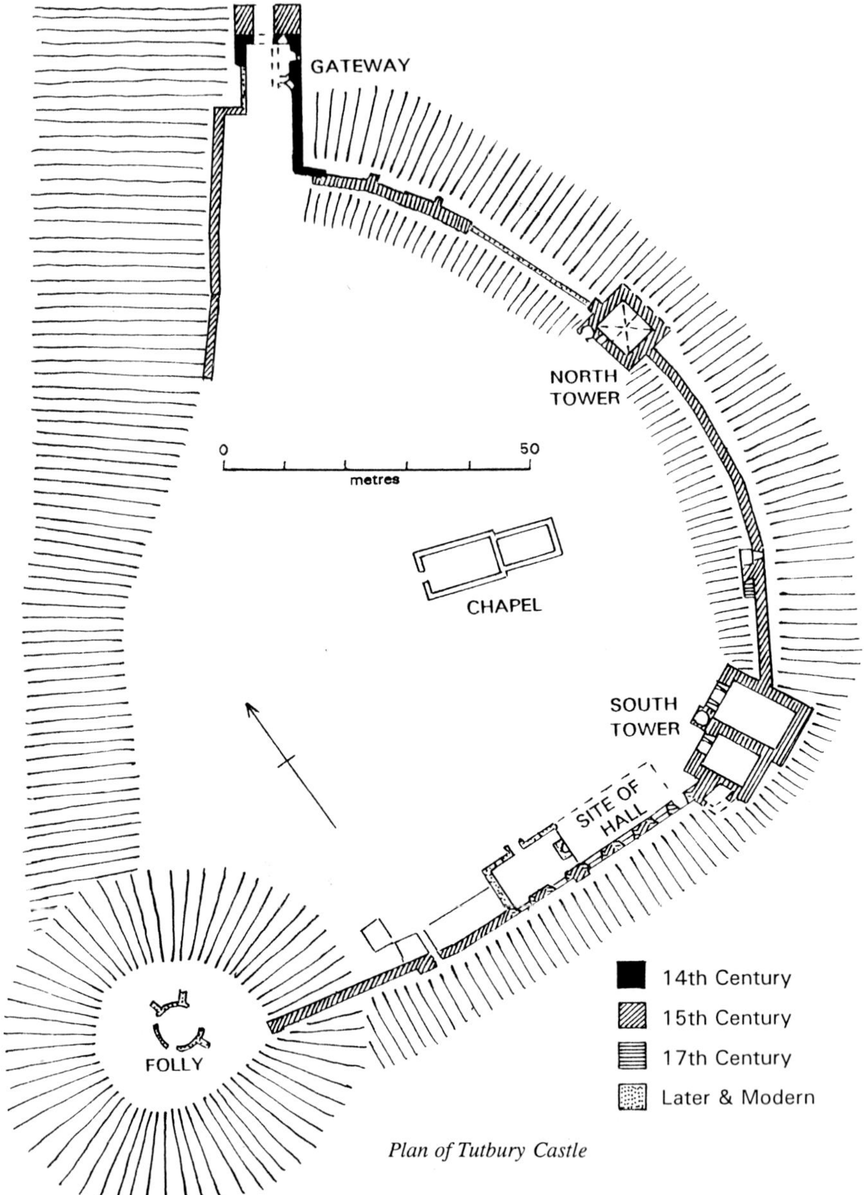

Plan of Tutbury Castle

Repairs were finally put in hand in 1561 and further work was carried out later to make the castle suitable for the incarceration of Mary, Queen of Scots, then under the charge of the Earl of Shrewsbury. She was accommodated in the medieval apartments from February until June 1569, the hall and chamber being subdivided with wainscotted partitions to make them more amenable to her. After short stays at Wingfield and Coventry, Mary returned to Tutbury for the first half of 1570.

In 1585 Mary was again at Tutbury under the charge of Sir Ralph Sadler, Chancellor of the Duchy of Lancaster. He stayed in the old apartments where Mary had previously been, and she was accommodated on the upper floor of a freestanding range which once stood to the south of the North Tower. She complained of the stench of a nearby privy without a drain that was emptied only once a week, and of her only privacy being in two small rooms with windows only facing the "dark surrounding walls". Sir Ralph did what he could to make life tolerable for Mary, taking her riding and hawking, but in April he was replaced by Sir Amyas Paulet, a Puritan who was stricter with the captive queen. He took up residence in the rooms over the gateway so as to oversee the approaches and observe persons entering the castle.

In the 1590s the outer gateway of the lower court was reported almost roofless, and the North Tower was badly cracked. Probably some repairs were made since James I visited Tutbury several times to enjoy hawking in Needwood Forest. In the 1630s his son Charles I had the medieval main apartments replaced by a new two storey range for which large new windows were pierced through the old curtain wall. Charles was at Tutbury in 1634 and on other occasions, and the castle was garrisoned for him in 1642, withstanding a short siege the following year. Charles and his nephew Prince Rupert were at Tutbury in 1645, but in 1646 the castle was surrendered to a Parliamentary force after a three week siege, and the defences were slighted in 1647.

Some of the accommodation at the castle was patched up in 1662 and leased to the Duke or Ormonde. From 1681 until 1864 the castle was leased to the Vernon family. A new house, incorporating some older materials, was built beside the site of the medieval hall in the 1750s, and follies were erected on the tops of the motte and the South Tower. Recent excavations have shown that the inner part of the eastern rampart is a landscaping feature of this era raised over the debris of the slighted curtain wall and the remains of buildings abutting the inner side. The new house was altered and extended in the 19th century and is still used by the resident caretaker. The Duchy carried out repairs to the ruins in 1832, and the system of charging fees from visitors to help pay for the upkeep of the site was introduced as early as 1847.

The chapel, Tutbury

Tutbury Castle has a D-shaped inner bailey with a mound at the south end, a steep drop to the river on the straight NW side,, and a deep and wide ditch around the other sides. The original approach was up the deep and wide gully dividing the two large outer enclosures on the east and NE sides, the latter now being a visitors car park. The other is currently a field but was used as a garden in the time of Mary, Queen of Scots. The present approach from the town is from the south and skirts the outer edge of the main ditch. It leads up to the gatehouse, a rectangular tower 11m by 8m externally with solid rectangular turrets added in front of it in the 15th century. The entrance arch is asymmetrically placed so as to allow the passageway to be flanked by a narrow room for a guard or porter on the south side. Only one upper storey remains but there is evidence that there were originally at least two.

The curtain wall from the gatehouse to the North Tower, and then onwards via a small turret and stair to the South Tower, now only stands 1.5m high. The first section south of the gateway shows signs of needing repeated rebuilding and repair, presumably because of poor foundations. The North Tower measures 10.6m by 9.m externally. It has a vaulted basement now almost buried in the rampart and having its own entrance direct from the court. A second entrance gives onto the foot of a spiral stair in a square turret up to the self contained suite of three fine upper rooms with large windows towards the court and latrines in the SE corner. These chambers are now very ruined but the turret stands almost to its original height.

The North Tower, Tutbury

The gatehouse at Tutbury

The South Tower, Tutbury

The South Tower is a double tower with the western part similar in design and size to the North Tower, whilst the eastern part is rather larger. Although probably intended to dominate the town and provide pairs of rooms on each of two or three upper storeys, the building seems to have been finished off its present height with just one set of rooms above cellars which were intended to be vaulted. Lintels for the fine fireplaces of the upper rooms were ordered in 1449. Close to the west is the site of the block of the range of the 1630s on the site of the medieval hall, beyond which is the brick house of the 1750s with a well over 36m deep in front of it. In the middle of the court are foundations of a Norman chapel consisting of a nave with a west doorway and a chancel which has perhaps been lengthened later. These were revealed by excavation in the 1950s. It is known that foundations of a round tower keep lie about two thirds of the way along the NW side of the court from the gatehouse but nothing is currently visible of this enigmatic building shown on the drawing of c1560.

Fanciful view of Tutbury Castle drawn c1560

WALSALL MANOR SP 001984 F

The first house on this site may have been built in King John's reign, when William le Rous created a park in this area. The moat which survived until recently, however, was dug either in 1338-9 when the two manors of Walsall were reunited in the hands of Ralph, Lord Basset, d1343, or in the mid 1380s when there is a mention of 543 cartloads of stone being delivered for a castle which Sir Ralph Basset was intending to build in support of his kinsman the Earl of Warwick against Richard II. The castle was not built, at least in its intended form, although in 1388-9 a moated mansion here was given a new drawbridge and a latrine, and the wooden gates were strengthened with iron plates. Further maintenance was carried out in 1396.

Under a settlement of 1339 Walsall passed upon Sir Ralph Basset's death in 1390 to Thomas Beauchamp, Earl of Warwick. As there was no resident lord (since the Earl had many other seats) the manor house was soon abandoned, and in 1438-9 the moat is recorded as being leased as a fishery. The house had disappeared by 1576, and c1870 the northern part of the moat was filled in and built upon. The rest of the moat contained water until the 1970s, when it was mostly filled, leaving just a shallow depression around the flats then built within it as adjuncts of the nearby hospital. Excavations in 1973-4 found that the original manor house was undefended and appeared to have been let out as a site for metal working before being later reconstructed as a moated residence.

WESTON JONES MOTTE SJ 768243

By a stream NE of the hamlet of Weston Jones is a low and worn down motte.

WEST BROMWICH OLD MANOR HOUSE SP 005943 V

This building was discovered to be an important timber framed house just in time to be saved from demolition. It has now been renovated and made into a restaurant. The house was erected by the Marnham family, holders of this part of the manor from 1275 until c1415. William Freebody is thought to have added the cross-wings in the 1430s. The gateway was built by Walter Stanley c1600, the section of moat in front then being filled in to make a forecourt. The rest of the moat was filled in c1700 but it has now been cleared out and refilled with water. The Skeltons purchased the house in 1626 and sold it in 1720 to the London merchant Sir Samuel Clarke.

WOLSELEY HALL SK 034204

In 1469 Edward IV licensed Ralph Wolseley to crenellate his house here in the Trent Valley between Colwich and Rugeley, but it is not known if anything was subsequently constructed as a result of this. The present hall does not appear to be of any great age, although the Wolseley family have lived here since at least the 11th century until modern times. The pool to the west may be a relic of a former moat.

WOLVERHAMPTON OLD HALL SO 719984

The name Old Hall Street is a reminder of the large mansion built by the Levesons c1550 in what was then open land outside the town. It had a brick walled court about 60m square with a wet moat outside it. The hall was sold in 1715, and, with the upper storey removed, was used as a Japanning works until it was demolished in 1883. The moat itself survived at least until the 1830s. The Adult Education College and the cinema and library stand on the site.

WYCHNOR MOAT SK 175159

Beside the canal to the south of the church are three dry arms of the surrounding moat of what was described in Henry VIII's reign as a ruinous old mansion subject to flooding.

OTHER EXTANT MOATED SITES IN STAFFORDSHIRE

ACTON TRUSSELL SJ 936176 Part of a circular wet moat by Manor Farm is probably a relic of the manor house of the Trussell family.
ALLEYS LANE SJ 844177 Slight traces visible of rectangular moat.
ASHMORE BROOK SK 096111 Fragment of wet moat by stream in valley.
ASHMORE PARK SJ 958018 Dry rectangular moat lies beside a shopping precinct.
ASTON BY STONE SK 924316 Some remains of moat around the hall.
BAGOT'S BROMLEY SK 066259 Remains of moat and a monument mark the site of the former manor house of the Bagot family.
BLAKENHALL SK 172182 Rectangular moat to the north of the hall.
BLITHEWOOD SJ 991365 Square platform with two concentric dry moats.
BLYMHILL GRANGE SJ 811120 Well preserved dry rectangular moat.
BOODEN FARM SJ 862198 Parts of a wet moat remain around the house.
BROCKENHURST SJ 824118 Parts of two moats remain south of the farm.
BURNHILL GREEN SJ 787008 Small damaged moated site behind a row of houses.
CASTLECHURCH SJ 897215 Worn down dry moat west of Stafford Castle.
CHARNES OLD HALL SJ 784340 Sections of a wet moat remain around the hall.
COMBERFORD SK 192073 Traces of the moat remain to the east of the house.
COMPTON PARK SO 806836 Slight traces remain of a former moat at the farm.
DOSTHILL SP 211000 Some remains survive of a partly wet rectangular moat.
ELFORD PARK SK 190123 Part of the moat remains to the north of the house of the 1760s. Part of the drawbridge was dug up in the late 18th century.
ESSINGTON HALL FARM SJ 951035 Rectangular moat, now partly filled in.
GAYTON SJ 978284 Most of the oval wet moat still remains around the house.
GORSTY HILL SK 109289 Square, tree-covered platform with wet moat.
HAGLEY HALL SK 042180 The large wet moat at Rugeley is probably the site of the house burnt in the 14th century and its successor.
HARLASTON SK 214110 Slight remains of a moat to the north of the church.
HARTWELL FARM SJ 917390 Remains of a moat lie beside the farm.
HAYGATE SP 053981 This dry rectangular moat near a house may be a relic of Sir Robert Stephenson's 14th century house.
HILDERSTONE SJ 957347 A moated platform lies some distance south of the hall.
HILTON SJ 952052 Two arms of a wet moat lie beside an 18th century house.
HOLLYBUSH FARM SJ 965064 There are remains of a rectangular wet moat.
KINGSLEY SK 007471 Remains of a large dry rectangular moat.
KNIGHTLY DALE SJ 816237 Part of a rectangular dry moat remains in a field.
LEA MANOR SJ 749421 A moat lies to the NW of the hall.
LITTLE ONN HALL SJ 840156 There are traces of ashlar work at the small moat by the house.
LONGCROFT SK 150200 Traces remain of a moat mostly filled in during the 1790s.
LUTLEY SO 816884 The rectangular moat is incomplete and partly ploughed down.
MAPLE HAYES SK 102101 This is a small but well preserved dry square moat.
MARCHINGTON WOODLANDS SK 041296 A quadrangular wet moat lies in a field.
MAYFIELD SK 143453 A small round wet moated enclosure remains on a ridge.
MOAT FARM SK 160304 There are some traces of a moat around the farm.

Dry moat in field near Lichfield

MOAT HILL SK 136246 Part of a moat remains to the south of the farmhouse.
MOAT HOUSE SJ 954030 Until c1930 a cottage stood on the platform of the rectangular moat which is probably "Le Mot" mentioned in 1321.
MOAT HOUSE BRIDGE SJ 930074 Two arms of a wet moat beside a canal bridge.
MOAT HOUSE, LONGDON SK 077139 There are slight remains of the east and south arms of a moat.
NEWBOROUGH SK 076471 Rectangular moat north of the house now nearly dry.
OULTON SJ 965335 Remains of a moat in a field between Oulton and Garshall.
PAYNSLEY HALL SJ 986380 There are remains of a moat around the hall.
PENKRIDGE SJ 936135 In a field are traces of three arms of a former moat.
PERTON COURT SO 860986 Only a fragment of the moat still survives.
RANTON ABBEY SJ 839244 Around the abbey precinct are traces of a moat.
RANTON HALL SJ 847244 There are remains of a moat around the hall.
RIBDEN SK 076471 Above a house is a small square platform with a dry moat.
SANDON SJ 956295 There is a wide wet moat around the house with an outer moat on the west side.
SHERHOLT LODGE SK 164206 There are slight remains of a moat beside the farm.
SIMFIELDS SJ 921469 The moat around this boggy rectangular platform is now mostly silted up.
THORNTREE HOUSE SK 086303 Traces of two moated rectangular platforms.
WATER EATON SJ 905113 West of the farm buildings are slight tracers of a moat.
WESTON PARK SJ 816098 A rectangular moat lies in woods SE of the house.
WILLOUGHBRIDGE SJ 743393 This is a fairly well preserved rectangular dry moat.
WOODEND SK 176266 A dry rectangular moat lies behind the farmhouse.
WOOD HALL FARM SJ 855037 Around a garden are three arms of a wet moat.
YOXALL SK 143188 Damaged moat by the bridge may go back to the 13th century when William Ferrers, Earl of Derby gave land to the clerk Roger de Yoxall.

FURTHER READING

The History and Antiquities of Staffordshire, Stebbing Shaw, 1798
The Buildings of Staffordshire, Nikolaus Pevsner, 1974
A History of Staffordshire, M.W.Greenslade and D.G.Stuart, 1965
The Victoria County History of Staffordshire, several volumes.
Norman Castles in Britain, Derek Renn, 1968
Medieval Newcastle-under-Lyme, T.Pape, 1928
Transactions of the North Staffordshire Field Club
Transactions of the South Staffordshire archeological and Historical Society
Transactions of the Birmingham and West Midlands Archeological Society.
William Salt Archeological Society Annual Transactions
Biddulph Historical Society Publications Medieval Archeology Country Life